The Body Now

Birthing the "Yes" Collective

Alana Shaw

BALBOA
PRESS

A DIVISION OF HAY HOUSE

Balboa Press books may be ordered through booksellers or by contacting:

Balboa Press
A Division of Hay House
1663 Liberty Drive
Bloomington, IN 47403
www.balboapress.com
1 (877) 407-4847

Print information available on the last page.

ISBN: 978-1-5043-7367-8 (sc)
ISBN: 978-1-5043-7368-5 (e)

Balboa Press rev. date: 05/01/2017

This book is dedicated to my children, Matthew, Andrea, Cassandra, Norah, Lucas, Aaron, and Morgan, and to my grandchildren, Tobias, Benjamin, Jayda, Lila, Margaret, Elias, Caitlin, and Sage, who have each been, in their own way, my greatest teachers, my deepest joy, and the basis for my enthusiastic belief in the beauty and magic of the unfolding time ahead.

Contents

Music Resources

Find Collection of Songs for Community
Singing at www.turningthewheel.org/songs

About the Author

Acknowledgements

I am deeply indebted to Khiri Lee, who read the first few drafts of this book and skillfully gave her very wise feedback all along the way. Her encouragement and her belief in the work have been a constant inspiration to me.

And there would be no book without the very experienced, intelligent, and patient editing and kind encouragement of Ann Bremner, who just kept showing up whenever I needed her and bringing her many years of professional knowing and personal wisdom to the process.

And, all of this work in both books evolved because of so many amazing folks who came to work with us and bring their love to the children in the schools and after-school programs. It is not possible to develop a model for working with people without people to work with!

Hundreds of volunteers have joined us and shared their ideas and feedback and a core of very dedicated facilitators have emerged over the years of doing this work. All of these folks have traveled extensively with TTW, working with populations as diverse as differently-abled youth and women in prisons.

I cannot express enough gratitude to this team of facilitators. There would be no book and no Turning the Wheel without them.

Daley Ackerman, Tanja Asmus, Lulu Delphine, Morgan Fox, Holly Hubbard, Lizzi Juda, Khiri Lee, Andy MacDonald, Stephanie Merrick Mitchell, Amy Millennor, Suzanne Palmer, and Perry Smith.

The folks you see above have been working with TTW for 15 to 25 years, and have become master facilitators of the work on every level; from their amazing facilitating in the field with youth and adults to the way they live their own lives. They are a very dedicated and hardworking group, who give tirelessly of themselves and their skills over and over again. You can learn more about them and our programming on our web site: www.turningthewheel.org.

My deep thanks also to:

Laurie Clark, Holly Lewis, Dodi Jackson, and Rick Silva, and Ed Huston, who have supported this work tirelessly in a myriad of ways for many years, from facilitating youth and building sets, to endless design, to beautiful performing and managing the data base!

And to:

Georgia Rose Park, Sarah Grieco, and Elizabeth Yochim, who were dedicated and significant players in building our story and have moved on to take the work into their own lives in creative ways, leaving us with a legacy of their wisdom and good energy to carry forward.

And as always, I feel such deep gratitude to all of my teachers, and I am especially grateful for and indebted to the community of women who have held me, encouraged me, and guided me through the last 45 years of my life: Elaine Yarbrough, Bernice Hill, Nancy Spanier, Kathlyn Hendricks, and the late Barbara Sternberg and Eloise Ristad.

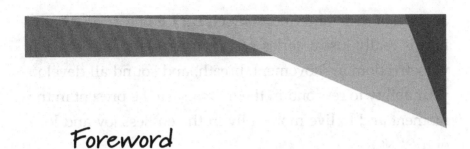

Foreword

My intention with this book is to be a part of the rising movement in the global soul's journey to create healthy, loving, thriving communities everywhere. These communities will support and nurture all of us and all of the children on this planet into strong and empowered, compassionate, and innovative contributors to the new world that is emerging right before our very eyes.

Specifically, I am passionate about getting all of you out into the world around you facilitating joyful, loving play, and creating accepting, loving communities. And to do that well, we have to do our own work; clean up our own stories on an ongoing basis, so we are living the model we are bringing to our communities. This book will guide you through the personal and the community "how to" of facilitating this well-being through creative, embodied art forms, from singing and dancing to word poems and spirit boxes.

Setting Yourself Up for Success

The exercises in this book are all different ways to enter into relationship with your body, and they are based primarily on movement improvisation, so you could really start with any one of them and find yourself back home in your body. Life is really just a series of improvisations, and finding your freedom in movement, breath, and sound all develop your ability to respond in the moment—to be present in the moment and to live more fully in the endless joy and love of the "NOW."

The model we have developed through 30 years of teaching over 100,000 youth and adults is one very significant piece of the puzzle for human evolution and well-being. It is a model that integrates well into teaching and facilitating your existing groups, and it is a gentle and profound path for pursuing your own independent development. It is not the only path but certainly one of them, and one that has the power to reshape our collective future. Endless possibilities open up when the body opens up—returning and awakening our life force, our vitality, and our creativity.

Some of the explorations in the book are tender and intimate and can be a little edgy, so it is good, as you begin, to do them yourself before you facilitate others. Even better, you can invite a friend to do them beside you, using the audio tracks available online to guide you both. Then you can check in at the end if you wish, quietly supporting each other with some good listening attention. The audio recordings that augment the descriptions in the book are available for many of the journeys at no charge online at www.turningthewheel.org/audio. This makes it possible for you to go back and forth between doing them alone and doing them in groups.

Some of the exercises only work as group forms, so you would need to invite a group of friends over to play with you for an evening, or maybe your book group, church group, recovery group, or your family would play. You may already be facilitating groups in which you can incorporate these forms once you have tried them out. In the past 30 years, I have used these forms and variations of them with incredibly diverse populations, including everyone from differently-abled groups to corporations, from teens to elders, and from severely underserved communities to the very privileged.

I am assuming that if you are reading this book, you already know quite a lot about yourself and that the individual exercises will be a pleasure for you, as you get a chance to gently deepen your knowing of your own inner landscape. I imagine that you will quickly be ready to take this work to your own groups, or ready to join our teacher certification program and begin teaching with us across the country.

Ultimately this work was created to be experienced and facilitated in groups. The depth of impact is exponentially increased when others are taking the journey with us in the room. The oneness of our molecular beings means that we are all taking each other's journeys as we take our own. The universality of our seeking and wanting and reaching and being is what makes that work so well. We really come alive in that field of evolutionary exploration as we support each other.

In that context, it is also very important to stay in touch with your own physical body when doing any improvisational work, let alone the kind of transformational journeying you are entering here. This includes drinking enough water, eating well, sleeping enough, and taking warm baths after a long day of moving. Taking care of our physical bodies is a big step into self-love.

Taking care can also mean creating time to integrate what you have been exploring on a feeling level, like taking walks in nature and making space for a quiet meditative time to journal or to check in with your body and your heart. Maybe you would like to find a friend to be a good listener, a loving witness to your journey. Asking for support and good attention is another way that we can love ourselves.

Setting Your Participants Up for Success
As you get to know this way of facilitating more and more, what is needed to support the work, and what makes it easeful and effective for you will emerge.

For example, finding a good improvisational musician—someone who will follow your group as they travel through their interior story—is a tremendous gift to the work. An intuitive and spontaneous musician can track the mood of the room and decide in each moment whether the music should be deep or light, slow or fast, sacred or silly, or quiet or boisterous.

We always mix some writing and art projects into the flow of the day if we are doing a daylong or weekend workshop. Such projects provide some rest for folks who are not used to being on their feet so much and let people who are auditory or visual learners have some time in their preferred learning styles.

In addition to the writing exercises sprinkled through this book, I have put some easy and fun art projects in the "Resources" section at the end. They can be easily integrated into your teaching symbolically. Examples include writing a love postcard to yourself and decorating the front, creating a treasure box to protect or honor the magic pieces of yourself, or making a magic wand of empowerment.

The "Facilitation Suggestions" that accompany many of the exercises share insights and ideas from our own workshops and groups. It is also always good to remind your participants and yourself to drink plenty of clean water, bring healthy snacks, and wear comfortable clothing.

One simple piece that we learned is how important it is to find a beautiful and comfortable space to hold your classes or workshops in. This includes a clean bathroom, which we sometimes forgot to check, nice lighting, and a place where participants can eat a snack and get some fresh air on their breaks.

And most important, I always remind participants that they should take care of themselves and their bodies and not do anything that feels uncomfortable to them. We are teaching ourselves and others to listen to our body signals, to pay attention to the messages from our bodies, so we want to be sure we apply that in our workshops as well.

Join Our Teams and Make a Difference in Your Community
Turning the Wheel has three ways that we reach out into our communities and you would be welcome to join us in any one of those ways any time.

1. The first path is our outreach to youth all across the country, giving youth who are primarily invisible in our communities thousands of hours of positive attention, helping them rebuild their self-esteem, and fostering their creative thinking so they can create more effective choices for themselves and become confident and innovative contributors to their communities.

Our teen mentoring program trains and hires the older kids to work with us in the grade schools where they learn that they can have an impact and make a difference, and where they are empowered as leaders.

We create an environment where the brains of our young people can literally rewire for a better life. Research has established that improvisational movement and creative spontaneous activity help to develop our brains' ability to respond freely in non-patterned ways to our environment, which is a must for youth who need a fresh start.

Over the past 30 years, we have created a vibrant and dynamic certification program that combines evolving and deepening into your own soul's journey with all the skills and mentoring needed to bring that magic to your community.

You can become a certified TTW facilitator and be part of helping to create new beginnings, new reference experiences, and new lives for literally thousands of kids and teens as they discover a new idea of how to live in positive relationship to themselves, their families and their communities. (See www. turningthewheel.org/certification.)

2. Our fastest growing outreach is to all of the adults that work with our youth and that create the communities and families our children grow up in: educators, caregivers in after-school programs and in homes, supervisors, therapists, parents, grandparents, extended families, etc.

Join us for a workshop for a day or for a week of "The Body Now" magic and find your own deep "yes" to yourself, as you discover and remember joyful ways to live and interact in your life.

Learn how to share those discoveries with your family and friends in your own workshops or in partnership with other members of the Turning the Wheel team. Our circle is always growing and we welcome you to join us. We will mentor and support you into your version of this very potent and developed model we have created.

3. We co-create original touring performance pieces that are professionally crafted, staged, and presented in cities across the country. These pieces bring together participants from all parts of a community, some who would never encounter each other otherwise. Our mingling includes everything from socioeconomic and racial diversity to age and ability diversity.

You can dance and sing in these pieces, help create them, build and install sets, create costumes, write and record text, help create the video footage, volunteer to drive teens and elders, mentor teens through the process, play games with the little ones while they wait and on and on. You can also simply come and see these spectacular collaborative creations and clap loudly!

Birthing the "Yes" Collective

I invite you to take a journey with me into finding, remembering, creating, inventing, practicing, and committing to a new way of standing on the earth, one that is connected to every living thing on the earth and driven absolutely by a deep and loving "yes."

We do not have to be stopped or stuck anywhere. Our very dynamic brains and our ever-changing, moving body will keep us dancing into the next moment. We are constantly in a state of becoming, moment to moment, body to body.

I know you can create your own future, and your own happiness, no matter what or where you come from or what you have experienced in your life. I know because I have done it myself and because I have facilitated thousands of others to find their way to a new life as well. You are not limited by your old stories, only blessed ultimately by the wisdom they bring and the ways in which they profoundly deepen your own compassion for others.

Alana Shaw

We already know everything we need to know about living joyful, easeful, peaceful lives together on the earth. There is no external system that can tell us how to thrive or be happy or how to manifest ourselves and our gifts. Our bodies have all that information and our hearts and souls are ready. The only question we need to ask is are we willing to recognize and express who we are at our deepest, most-expanded level in a way that supports and celebrates our unique and absolutely crucial gifts. The very survival of our earth depends on the manifestation of those gifts.

In my personal search for new possibilities, I have been blessed with a truly magical piece of the healing puzzle. Now, 49 years later, I want to share with you what I know about the wisdom of the body and how it came to be my vision of "The Body Now."

In this book you will find a gathering of ideas, stories, and movement-based exercises that will help you remember and reconnect to what you already know, inviting you to take the next steps on your journey into embodied wholeness. Those steps, which really are about falling in love with yourself over and over again, will gently and easily send you on your way to manifesting more and more of your own true story.

Loving ourselves wholeheartedly, and then creating loving, accepting, and healing environments for others, is certainly one of the answers to every question on the table today. I have been enthusiastically bringing this message to communities across the country for over 30 years. It is now rising up to the surface of the collective consciousness, and change is rapidly following everywhere I look.

Your authentic story, the story that is yours alone, is an essential piece of the puzzle for the well-being of all of us. The vibrations from your loving integrity move out into the collective unconscious of the world in vibrant circles of healing energy. Your magic is crying out to be brought forth. It has been there for a long time, waiting for your conditioned story to surrender to your authentic being. Let's just skip the old stories completely and head out into the world, the world we can create with our brains right now!

Now is the time to jump into this story of unbridled loving energy for yourself and others, and to add your own contribution to the unfolding of all the possibilities that come with this magical force for good.

Creating Your Own Story

I began on the floor with the back of my father's hand imprinted on my face. I know the story of the abused child intimately. I lived it consistently, on every level of my being, for the first 17 years of my life. I know the very day that story began to change for me, though it took many years to manifest.

I can still remember the light on the day that I knew I would find a new story: sunlight coming in through the back bedroom window, shining a pathway hopefully across the bare wood floor. I was looking out of that window into the apple orchard.

My father's brutality was trained on my brothers instead of on me this time. I sat in the corner, helpless, as tears flowed without sound down my face. I was trying to hold the very difficult feelings of fear and sadness for my brothers and guilty relief that it wasn't me this time—the terror of powerlessness for all of us.

I remember praying desperately for the angels to come and save us. I remember seeing those angels on the ground like huge dead birds that could no longer fly or believe.

I remember a sudden and strange flash of light, perhaps the sun shifting in the window—and hearing words, words from somewhere deep inside me.

"I will stop this. This has to stop."

A toughness was born in that moment, a determined reach for survival, a strength that grew. I was little, maybe five or six years old, shaking as I watched my father beating my brothers, and I believe that in this both traumatic and astounding moment, I made the decision, consciously and unconsciously, that I would dedicate my life to rescuing all the children of the world, and to creating a world where no child would ever be hurt again.

I suppose I was probably possessed in a way, tapping into the collective unconscious, tapping into an idea that was cognitively too sophisticated for me to really understand, while at the same time I was being so clearly called to my life's work. In that very moment, I believe my deep body commitment became fiercely rooted to the well-being and happiness of children everywhere and to whatever it would take to make that happen.

So I began very young to fight hard for my "self" and my survival, and for the rights of my brothers and sisters and friends and the other kids in my school, which in the beginning only brought me more abuse. Neither my family environment nor my school classrooms offered a fertile place for my zealousness or my vision. I was not able to heal my father's pain at age eight or to be in charge of my teachers, let alone whole school systems.

I vacillated between being fully embodied and knowing clearly that what was happening was not right, and leaving my body completely, hovering above and watching to escape the physical pain of the abuse.

In my early 20s, guided by my personal journey out of a life defined by abuse and an ongoing struggle to survive, I began reaching out with movement and ritual to women in safe houses and their children, who were caught in a similar cycle to the one I had escaped from. These women responded to the lifeline I had discovered with so much eagerness and willingness that I was encouraged to keep going, expanding the populations I played with and the ways in which I played.

Turning the Wheel

In 1989, after 20 years of experimenting with creative classes and gatherings for every imaginable population and studying with over 30 different teachers in workshops and classes, I founded a nonprofit corporation called Turning the Wheel Productions (TTW). Based in movement and the expressive arts, TTW is dedicated to directly helping our young people—one by one—recover their self-esteem and find their gifts, and to building healthy communities for them to interface with and safely grow up in.

In the last 27 years, we have touched the lives of more than 100,000 people in 15 cities and over 1000 schools and organizations. Our work has expanded to include workshops for educators, caretakers, corporations, and all manner of people looking for a healthy and joyful life.

Facilitating our most vulnerable youth into being contributing members of our society and building healthy communities around them are inextricably bound together. We have to heal and manifest our own integrity as we reach out to our youth, and we must form authentic connections and genuine partnerships with them to co-create positive possibilities for our future on the earth.

The youth we work with are making better choices for themselves and guiding those around them to do the same, replacing isolation and apathy with connection and action. They are listening to their bodies and taking cues from them. They are finding out that they can have an impact and that they can truly make a difference in their own lives and in the lives of others.

Our commitment is to bring to the youth, and to all of us who influence their well-being, the very powerful combination of listening and responding to their body wisdom, while owning and living into their innately good and loving essence.

The body is our most fundamental mechanism of change. Moving, listening, playing, and responding to that body is the quickest and most direct path to joy and to our most authentic selves. When we are moving, we use every single part of our brain—it all lights up. We activate the whole neurological system.

Further, recent research shows that only 20 minutes of moving elevates the nitric oxide levels in the body for 24 hours. Nitric oxide is the über transmitter in the body, releasing beta-endorphins, prolactin, oxytocin, serotonin, and dopamine: all feel-good allies in the body. My dream is that every man, woman, and child on the earth will start their day with 20 minutes of exercise and then spend the next 24 hours feeling good and manifesting their dreams.

"The Body Now"

In collaboration with an incredible team of truly brilliant and dedicated TTW facilitators, I have created an improvisational movement-based model for healing and expressing and creating that is not only effective but also revolutionary. It is a four-step mandala of healing for moving into joy and self-love called "The Body Now" (see illustration on p. 45).

It includes many exercises and moving journeys to support you along the way on your path to becoming a clear and open-hearted channel for unconditionally loving energy so you can facilitate and create environments that are innately healing for yourself and for others.

This model grew out of knowing it could be done—out of having done it for myself. More importantly, it came out of learning, on the ground, what could make a truly sustainable difference for our participants.

In the later chapters in the book, we will go through the steps and exercises on "The Body Now" mandala. You can try out the exercises yourself first, using the online auditory guides (www.turningthewheel.org/audio). Then you can integrate the visualizations in the book into your own healing or meditation practice, your workshops or events, your family reunions, or as play with your children and grandchildren. You can gather friends and explore your stories together, supporting and taking turns guiding each other through the exercises, manifesting your sacred gifts together.

And as you live more and more into your commitment to come from that clear channel, you can take your gifts and loving kindness further out into the world. You inevitably will meet challenges as you reach out that take you back to clearing your own vessel again. I view this as the ongoing opportunity to keep evolving as a human being, continuing to discover and heal more parts of ourselves us that want our attention and love.

This need to give some loving attention to a part of myself is often triggered by seeing aspects of my own journey in someone in the group. As I return to the healing cycle on "The Body Now" mandala and come into a loving relationship with this triggered part, I get to deepen my personal healing one more level and at the same time to create another level of clarity in my container so I can bring even more loving acceptance to the folks I am facilitating.

Recently I had a particularly poignant experience of seeing myself in a young man who came to dance in a performance with us. I knew as soon as he walked in the door he would make the shift—discover himself—in this room with this beautiful community of people who were ready to let him show up as his authentic self. He was ready to be seen.

Instead of reacting to his "rudeness," I opened a space in my heart for him and saw him already blooming. I didn't know his name, but I already knew him. I saw myself at his age: defensive, angry, confused, labeled as a troublemaker for sure, but with a subtle and very sweet willingness tucked just under the surface, and a very sharp mind and quick body waiting for a chance to show up, waiting to be seen.

This boy was middle school age and had a tough exterior already in place. Middle school is a very apt name, as the middle school children we work with are so "caught in the middle" between being taken care of and protected in the grade school environment and not being old enough to take care of themselves like the high school youth. They are suspended between two worlds and always a little lost and vulnerable. If they have parents or a dedicated caretaker who takes an interest in them or who has time to spend with them, they are more likely to make this transition successfully.

Unfortunately, many of the youth we work with do not have anybody who knows where they are or what they are doing. The parents or other caregivers do love their kids and care about where their kids are, but they are often just not in a position to do anything about it because they are working double or triple shifts just to keep food on the table, or because of their own struggles with addictions, anger, poverty, single-parent isolation, violent relationships, depression or other mental and physical health issues and illnesses with no access to resources for medical care, to name only a few recurrent challenges.

When I was in middle school, which was then called junior high, the secretary in the principal's office had a special desk that she pulled up next to her desk for me when I was sent to the principal's office, sometimes more than once a day. She spoke lovingly to me and gave me cookies from her bottom drawer and sometimes even helped me with my homework. I suppose I partly got sent out of the classroom just to be with her, but I also knew I was "bad" and felt very ashamed that I just couldn't manage to be "good," which meant to remain silent in the face of injustice, unkindness, and rudeness by the teachers to the students.

Since I couldn't do anything about the violence in my own home, I was always championing somebody else in the classroom, and then being told to leave—and I soon became known as a troublemaker. I was most definitely troubled, and from a very troubled family, but not a "troublemaker." Although I often came to school with many visible bruises on my face and arms, no interventions were made or questions asked. In my desperation to be seen and make up for my "badness," I developed a strong overachiever stance, powered by adrenaline and anxiety. I excelled in swimming, ran track in state meets, sometimes made straight As, played concert piano, and even won a regional drawing contest in my art class. But all of that was rarely acknowledged or seen, at home or in school.

I was a classic example of how what you give attention to grows, and I got attention for being "bad," speaking out of turn, criticizing my teachers, expressing my anger inappropriately, refusing to cooperate, and just generally disrupting the classroom in any way I could. And when any teacher or staff member—like my art teacher or the principal's secretary—turned a loving light on me and saw my sweetness, my vulnerability, or my gifts, the transformation was instant. I would become myself, my essence would float up the surface, and I would settle quickly into focused attention and successful completion of any work offered.

In fact, I wanted to be "good" and to be liked by the teacher, and I wanted to succeed—so desperately that I would quickly transform into that overachiever. Looking back, it feels so clear that a greater force of love was watching over me and guiding me through, as I continued to send out messages, however awkwardly, of what I knew I wanted for myself and for others.

We have seen this happen over and over with the youth we work with, including the young man I mentioned above. He emerged as a strong leader and a very coordinated and creative mover, and brought both of those gifts to our project with joy. All of his teachers and his mother were astounded at his transformation, which really was just his true self showing up. The basic need of these young people to have impact—to have their "goodness" witnessed and to matter to somebody—is our ticket to bringing them back to themselves and to their success.

We most certainly need these young people as much as they need us. We need their success. We need their diversity of ancestry and all the ways of thinking and seeing that they bring. We need their leadership and their innovation. We need whole populations of empowered, innovative, creative youth to create this new quantum world we are just beginning to understand.

My dear friend Diana, whose vast wisdom has mentored and loved me through more than 40 years of my life, gave me a beautiful image for our work with communities in Turning the Wheel, which has been inspiring for me, as it is was reflected to me through nature. She was describing to me the amazing ecosystem of the "boundary waters." As I remember, she described "boundary waters" as a sort of improvisational nursery for the development of the ocean, a place where fresh water and salt water come together to create something new and where biodiversity is both remarkable and essential for the ongoing health of the earth.

As she spoke, I realized that at Turning the Wheel we are working in the "boundary waters" of our communities. As "boundary water" workers, we are committed to birthing our own evolution so that we can truly create a nursery—in an environment of huge diversity—for new stories to be born in the beautiful folks we are so privileged to learn and grow and play beside. It is out of this diversity that the ongoing health of the earth and all of us living on the earth will be achieved and sustained. I realized that innovation and creativity have historically and consistently happened in the boundary waters, whether giving birth to new forms of dance or new understandings of the mysteries of the cosmos.

This intersection of the fresh water with the salt water is a beautiful metaphor for the basic need for diversity, for the ongoing connection with each other, something that we all long for regardless of our differences. That connection to each other is birthed and maintained through finding our willingness to live in a fully embodied "Yes" to our connection to our own body wisdom, and to our feelings, our compassion, our generosity, our purpose, and ultimately to meaning, to spirit, to the earth, and to what is sacred for each of us.

What Does "Birthing the 'Yes' Collective" Mean?

In my most passionate and idealistic heart, "Birthing the 'Yes' Collective" means person by person, all across the world, we change all of our "no" answers to "yes" answers and watch the world story turn into one fabulous "yes," manifesting a joyful, open-hearted, co-created story.

Our model is based on finding this loving and accepting "yes" in your body. It is based on knowing when you are feeling it in your body and how to shift into a "yes" if you are not there. It is based on a willingness to find your unconditional "yes" to yourself and to all others. Like everything we do in Turning the Wheel, this model emerged over time as I journeyed out of my family history into health and into my own true story.

My body has been my guide through my whole life, teaching me all I needed to know and taking me down just the right paths all along the way, even when I didn't know it. The most beautiful parts of my life have come from listening to the messages my body was bringing to me instead of listening to my old internal stories or to the voices around me carrying hardwired cultural beliefs. No matter how it may look at first to ourselves, or to others around us who are steeped in the cultural norms, our body will never lie to us or guide us in the wrong direction.

When I was seventeen, I found out I was pregnant. At the time I was the student body leader of my high school and getting ready to graduate and attend Cornell College in Ithaca, New York, on a scholarship in the fall. My parents were obviously very upset and angry and wanted me to get an abortion in Sweden, a very expensive and complex process and the only safe option at that time.

They let me know that I had brought great shame on the family and that we needed to keep this horrible behavior a secret, even from my little sister, as she might follow in my misguided footsteps. My father called me a "whore" and a "slut," and told me that I would also be an adulteress ultimately, as that was the fate of young women who were promiscuous sexually. My mother cried ceaselessly and just kept saying that she had thought I was a good kid, and she just couldn't understand what had happened to me.

Once again my seeming tragedy become my salvation. I knew, when I listened to my body, that I really wanted the being inside me, and I decided to keep the baby and marry the boy I had become pregnant with, and leave home. Odd as it may seem, my reclaiming of the power of "yes" began with an actual birthing, the birth of this child when I was eighteen years old.

Being basically rejected by my very dysfunctional and abusive home was the best thing that could have happened to me. Though I was too young to have a child by the judgment of those around me, it was truly the beginning of my healing, the beginning of my first real happiness, and another very clear step on my journey to my authentic work on the earth.

For an eighteen-year-old, I was very grown up in some ways and very eighteen in others. But I had a very clear, full-body "yes" to the incredibly beautiful little baby boy, Matthew, who came to be in my life. This "yes" came with a clear commitment to learn what I needed to know to nurture this child in health and happiness, not realizing that I was seeking to nurture my own inner child at the same time.

I knew that there was virtually nothing to carry forward from my family in terms of how to raise a happy healthy child. I knew that everything that had been done in my family, I didn't want to do. This was a gift in so many ways, as my search for how to raise my own child began a lifelong search for how to do this for myself and ultimately for everyone else in my life.

The first answer came from my very wise pediatrician, Dr. Amer, who had known me since I was very young and had been a lifeline during my adolescent years, quietly loving and appreciating me every chance he got. When Matthew was born, he helped me get started breastfeeding him, much to the chagrin of the nurses at the hospital, who in those days were recommending bottle feeding as a much more measureable and consistent way to feed your baby.

He gave me his prescription for a happy child. He wrote it on his prescription pad and I can still see it today: "Loving and holding and rocking in a rocking chair," simple, but pure genius, which I followed religiously. He also recommended that I keep him on my body as much as possible with as much skin-to-skin touch as possible—radical advice for 1965.

He sent me to a wonderful organization called La Leche League, saying that he had never nursed a baby himself, but that he knew some people who had. In 1965, in Boulder, La Leche League was a incredibly loving group of young mothers who were breastfeeding their children, raising them in a kind and supportive environment, and helping other young mothers do the same.

I read every book in their lending library hungrily, all good books, and in the process came upon a book called *Summerhill: A Radical Approach to Childrearing*. The author, A. S. Neill, founded a school in England in 1921, called "Summerhill," with the philosophy that the school should be made to fit the child.

We set out to make a school in which we should allow children freedom to be themselves. In order to do this we had to renounce all discipline, all direction, all suggestion, all moral training, all religious instruction. We have been called brave, but it did not require courage. All it required was what we had—a complete belief in the child as a good, not an evil, being. Since 1921 this belief in the goodness of the child has never waivered. (New York: Hart Publishing Company, 1965, p. 4)

What a stunning and courageous stance to take in 1921 or even now. The need for this innovative and revolutionary approach is still as great today as it was then.

The specific direction that I remembered most from the book was that you could raise your children in an atmosphere and energy of absolute permission: all "yes," without ever saying "no." You simply let go of any ideas you had about what the child should do or not do, or be or not be, and let him or her grow up freely choosing their own pathway and freely exploring their environment. Though still a controversial idea more than 90 years later, we have seen literally hundreds of different successful educational and business models grow out of this philosophy.

Having been raised in a system of control, based on such deep and profound shame, and relentless physical and mental abuse, I was an instant convert—a true believer. And to this day, I guess in many ways, I still am. Matthew's birth combined with *Summerhill* and all those beautiful women committed to the health and happiness of their children landed the "how to" for my already lifelong vision: **to journey with others towards our wholeness and to return**

to our joyful authenticity, saving all the children along the way.

The first sentences of the vision statement of Turning the Wheel echo that influence.

Everything that we do in Turning the Wheel is an attempt to come back into relationship with our interdependence as human beings, and with the need for love, not control, to form the basis for how we live on the earth. We are passionately committed to building and sustaining transformative communities that are inclusive of all people, that nurture and love the children, and that reach for and model unconditional love and acceptance as the norm.

For the last 26 years, we have trained all of our facilitators in how to run a project in any environment, with any group of kids or adults, without saying "no" to anybody or to themselves, internally or externally. And the miracle is that it works, over and over again with every possible kind of person you can imagine, from the very challenged to the very privileged.

This concept of really believing in the innate goodness of every human and setting out to co-create with that goodness is an amazingly successful way to nurture humans into bringing their most productive positive sides back to themselves, to their families and to their communities. In a word, it works!

Changing to "Yes"

I awaken the love, sleeping deep in my cells, and feel the gentle caressing of my heart's knowing.

Let's explore what it means to live into a full body "yes," one where all of you feels energetically and enthusiastically aligned with your "yes."

It is truly transforming just to become conscious of how many times in a day, or even in an hour, we say "no" or "yes, but," with all of our qualifiers to ourselves and to each other. This can be anything from actually deciding you can't have what you want, to a litany of constant complaining, criticizing, and blaming others—all ways of saying no. For many of us, there are times when this combination of thoughts fills most of our time.

Our brains simply believe whatever we tell them. They are servant to our every whim, one immense and very responsive internal feedback loop. Every thought we have actually activates a series of responses in our bodies that result in our feeling exactly what we were just thinking. Given that we know that we have about 60,000 thoughts a day and that 90% of those are the same as yesterday, it probably is worth paying attention to what we are feeding our brains to repeat each day.

So how do we create a new story around these patterns? We begin by truly loving and appreciating this "no" part of ourselves, remembering when it saved us or kept us safe. We remember that it is a voice of our inner child that needs rocking and holding and loving until it relaxes into its essence and ease.

Embracing and loving all of who we are serves to restore our creativity and allows hundreds of possible "yes's" to float to the top. I am amazed over and over again at how many times what seems like it ought to be a "no," is just a "yes" in disguise. It so depends on how we are looking at our lives or the situation confronting us. We know we are interfacing with our body wisdom, our deeper knowing, when we are generating lots of options and opening to them as new perspectives and possibilities.

The late Paula Underwood, an Iroquois oral historian I studied with, once told me that in her native tribe they had a "Rule of Six." You could only move to the step of making a decision about anything when you had generated at least six different solutions that everyone involved was comfortable with. She maintained that once you got to six you could go on to hundreds, as you would have interrupted the "either this or that" pattern of thinking and activated your creative mind. Finding at least six possibilities that you can say "yes" to opens up the field, getting things moving, and it bypasses the reptilian brain, which wants a "yes" or a "no."

My youngest son experienced a very dramatic example of the power of the "Rule of Six." He was diagnosed with a rare kidney disease at age 13 and told he would need a kidney transplant within six months in order to live. His choice and our choice as a family to live outside the "either this or that" story of the kidney specialist delayed that transplant for 16 years. Once we opened up other ways of looking at what was happening in his body, our research netted us many more than six options for pursuing his health.

The very polarizing story of "either yes or no" is deeply embedded in our culture and will often shut down innovative and creative thinking before it evens get started, so it is a wonderful place to stay curious and very empowering to embrace a practice of generating options. It absolutely changes the lives of the youth we work with in amazingly quick ways—bringing new possibilities to them in as little as a few minutes.

Recently we were working with a group of high school kids doing theatre scenes in small groups with them. They were making up the improvised scenes based on the experiences they have had in their lives, which mostly centered around conflict and blaming. Our facilitators let them do this for a bit as they got used to the theatre form. They also found the humor in these scenes, which was good, as they found they could gently laugh at themselves and their lives.

After awhile, without any judgment of what the kids had been doing, the TTW facilitators suggested they try a new challenge and see if they could take the conflict scenes and move them into agreement by the end of the time allowed. What would they have to do to as a group, improvising in the moment, to bring their whole group into agreement— that is to move out of "either this or that"?

And every one of the groups did it. They learned a new possibility—to come to agreement—that many of them had never experienced. They were practicing the "rule of six" without knowing it. They now have a reference experience in their bodies of how successful and pleasant that felt. It was revolutionary for them to feel the ease with which they could find agreement and the good feelings they had about themselves and each other when they did. Needless to say their teachers were astounded and delighted, and opened up new places in their own hearts for the parts of the youth they had not witnessed.

"Yes Let's"

Try playing this fun exercise with a group and see what happens as you give everybody an opportunity to easily and joyfully practice generating lots of options and to practice saying "yes" to everything in the moment.

You can play this game at any gathering you can imagine, from your book group to your sister's wedding! It is so enlivening to hear ourselves playfully saying "yes" over and over with no consequences attached.

This is a game called "Yes Let's." We will all start walking in the room and anybody can call out an activity for us to do, like:

"Let's all skip,"
"Let's all jump up and down,"
"Let's all scratch our noses,"
"Let's all laugh," or

"Let's all stand still."

We all respond by saying "Yes Let's" and doing the activity that was called out until someone calls out another activity. Have fun. I will start.

When you are ready to end the exercise just say, *"Let's all make a circle,"* and you will have your group back.

Facilitation Suggestions
This is a quick and simple game to set up, a good warm-up for the body, and it only lasts about 10 minutes.

You may need to call out a few activities before the group gets brave enough to call some out, or have your facilitators keep it going until the participants get the idea. This needs to move along pretty quickly. Doing any one activity too long, like jumping up and down, can be hard physically on some of your group, and gets boring.

This is one of our favorite ways to begin a workshop or rehearsal or weekend retreat. It helps everybody come into their willingness to be present with the activities that are coming and gets everybody moving and laughing.

The idea is to teach the brain to say "yes" instead of "no": to wire the brain for "yes," to find our "yes" to all the people and new opportunities that are around us and, ultimately, to giving and receiving love most of the time.

The Magic of "Yes, And"

Some years ago an amazing woman from Canada taught me another way to explore this story of "yes" and "no." We have used it literally hundreds of times since then in our work in training facilitators and educators in Turning the Wheel. We call it simply "Yes, And."

This is a powerful tool to help all of us find our "yes." It is an opportunity to experience in our bodies what it is like to be supported by a clean and co-creative yes, and what it feels like in our bodies to be met with the solid wall of "no." It is also a chance to experience what it feels like to be met with the quiet, insidiously discouraging "yes, but" that we all too often receive from others and give to others, sometimes without realizing it, all in the name of being helpful.

For example, I learned that whenever I heard myself saying, internally or externally, "I was just trying to be helpful" that I had unconsciously moved into fixing someone else, and therefore I was innately criticizing them for who they were in that moment—a "yes, but" response for sure.

That realization has saved me from many hours of futile "fixing," and all the feelings of frustration and anger that go with trying to fix people who don't want to be fixed, who don't want to be made wrong for who they are right now, and who are not asking for my advice.

It usually goes something like this. My friend has yet another cold and I know she eats a lot of sugar. I would like her to feel better and not be sick so much. So I tell her about how eating sugar compromises the immune system and makes us vulnerable to the colds going around. Now she not only has a cold but also feels bad about herself and shamed for eating sugar.

My "yes, and" would look very different. I might ask her if I could bring her some soup to help her heal, or ask if I could pick up anything at the grocery for her. I might remind her that every one I know has had this cold and encourage her to rest and take care of herself. Most of all I would let go of my need to make her wrong and see what needed loving in me—maybe my fear of getting the cold—and then quietly loop some loving energy to her and be grateful that I am feeling healthy that day.

Even when folks seem to be asking for advice directly, they probably are not, and what they really want is to be listened to with no agenda and affirmed for the process they are in, regardless of what you may have to offer on the subject.

I once had a friend ask at what age you should stop nursing your baby. I immediately shared my opinion about that and what I knew to be important about long-term breastfeeding. It wasn't until I took a breath, and she got to speak her very defensive response, that I realized she was not asking a question at all, but simply wanting to be affirmed and supported in her decision to wean her baby that month.

Of course, there are still those somewhat humorous times that I can laugh at later, when I am certain that somebody really needs to know what I know about something: what you should eat, how you should exercise, how to speak to your children, how to teach your class, what plants to put in your garden, which supplements you need to be taking, just for starters. I know a lot of things.

I once even gave a friend money to go to a weight-loss program. She paid the money to the program and never attended the sessions. It was a clear and hard lesson for me in remembering that that nobody wants to be fixed—even if their life depends on it—and everybody wants to be appreciated and accepted for who they are!

The positive side of all of this is that my very enthusiastic little girl wants everyone to be happy. And happily, there is a way I can be helpful that protects me and protects my friends from feeling wrong. I can begin by asking them if they would like to know what I have to offer on a particular subject, which is a very different place to start and a significant shift for me from instant fixing.

To begin with, I have taken a breath and shifted my position in my body or I would not have been able to ask the question. The paradox is that, if I get that far—the breath and the movement—I will probably just listen and not need to offer any advice at all. Or maybe I will listen longer before offering advice, so I know what the real question is.

In that pause, I can notice if where I have gone is into criticism, into thinking that I know what they need to do, that I know what is "right" for them to do. If I feel that contraction in my body, the body stillness of fixing others, I can release that contraction on a very physical level, flow fluids into that contracted place, and restore movement. Then I can simply witness my friend in love, giving her good attention, and trusting that she will find her own good answers.

I think I have saved thousands of hours of wasted time and energy since I made the commitment to stop fixing others and just give them some good, loving, affirmative attention. The good news is that I now have all of that energy to put into manifesting what I want in my life and into activities and interactions where I can make a difference. I guarantee, nobody wants to be fixed. Everybody, including me, wants to be seen.

"Yes, And"

So here is the wonderful exercise I learned from my Canadian friend, which is always an astonishing experience in self-awareness and consistently empowering. We will explore the power of our own responses to others and how the response of others to us may be subtly controlling our decisions.

This process is honestly capable of moving a group from being mostly disconnected to finding deep loving connection in 30 minutes. It is the "yes, and" response that ultimately makes it safe and empowering for others to be in our circle. You can easily do this with a friend in your kitchen before guiding a group through the exercise.

Once your group is warm and relaxed into their bodies a bit, ask them each to choose a partner and find a place in the room and to stand facing each other. Now take a moment and have everybody think of something they really want to accomplish, a dream they have or an activity they want to try, or maybe a project they want to complete.

Once everybody has something to work with, you are ready to begin with the first step, which is experiencing and delivering the "no."

It is important to do a good demonstration of this here, as we are not used to owning our "no" outright, and it is also an opportunity for the whole group to really get the power of "no." So choose one of your assistants or co-facilitators to help you and let them tell you their dream and you just simply shut them down, very politely, with all the reasons why it is impractical and unrealistic and just isn't going to happen.

"Truthfully, I just don't think this is going to happen."
"We simply do not have the resources to pull that off."
"Our donors would not approve of this idea at all."
"This sounds totally impractical to me, and frankly, a little crazy."
"You are insane. Sometimes I wonder where you came from."
"I hate to say this, but I can't support you in this."
"I wonder why you are so obsessed with this idea."

It can actually be a little humorous in an odd way.

Then, in the same demo, repeat the conversation with your
body and sounds only. The dreamer is gesturing about their
dream and the listener is responding with a whole body no.
This will set the group up for the whole exercise and help
you move them through from one step to the next more
easily.

"No"

*So here we go. We will begin with saying "no" to each other and
see how that feels for us. One person will begin as the speaker and
the other will be the one to say no. I promise not to let this go on
too long. I will call freeze when it is time to stop and switch roles.
Does everybody know who is saying "no" first?*

OK, so here we go.

I don't let it go on too long—it can be a bit traumatizing.

After a few minutes say:

Pause.

*Now, still without talking—I promise to leave time for talking at the
end—change roles. If you were the one saying no, now you share
your dream or desire and your partner will tell you all the reasons
it is not a good idea, and why you will not succeed.*

Again, after a few minutes say:

Pause.

It is important to catch your group right at the freeze before they begin talking about the experience so they can experience the sensations in their bodies first.

Now, repeat the same conversation with the same roles, only doing it all with body gestures, adding sounds if you wish, just no words. So if you were the one telling your dream, tell it again with body gestures and sounds, and if you were the one saying "no," say "no" again with body gestures and sounds. You will probably both end up moving at the same time. I will call freeze again when it is time to pause and switch roles. Ready. Go.

After a few minutes, have your participants switch roles.

Now take a few minutes to talk about that experience and how it felt in your body. Where does your "no" come from in your body, and where do you receive the "no," where do you feel the sense of discouragement and give up. Just notice what happened in your body and share with your partner.

Now let's all shake that off and let it go before we go on to the next step.

Facilitation Suggestions

Once you let the group start it can be hard to get over the top so they can hear you say freeze. It is a high adrenaline experience, so it often gets charged and loud very quickly. You may need your musician to help with some strong drumbeats. I have even been known to get up on a chair!

You can set a timer for two or three minutes if you are doing this with a friend in your kitchen.

"Yes, But..."

The next step, "yes, but..." might be worse in some ways than "no." It is confusing and tricky, as it seems like you might be getting support but really you are not. It goes something like this:

"Yeah, I love your enthusiasm, but I have seen a lot of those projects fail pretty darn quickly."

"It's a great idea, but I doubt you could raise that kind of money in today's economy."

"Yes, I see the need and hear your desire to help, but reaching all those children would take a lot of people and a lot of money, not to mention the hard work."

"I understand your intentions are good, but I am not sure you have really thought this through all the way."

And on and on...

Again, it is important to do good demonstration of this with your co-facilitator to set the group up for success. One cue that helps is to suggest that they keep their responses short enough and pause enough that the other person can get in. I also tell them to feel free to interrupt—a sure sign you are in a "yes, but..." conversation with somebody.

This time we will take turns presenting the same dream but this time the responder will be saying "yes, but..." Again, one person will begin as the speaker and the other will be the one to say "yes, but..." I will call freeze when it is time to stop and switch roles.

OK, so here we go again.

After a few minutes (you might want to time this) say:

Pause.

Now, still without talking—I promise to leave time for talking at the end—change roles. If you were the one saying "yes, but..." now you share your dream or desire and your partner will tell you all the reasons that such a good idea probably will not succeed.

After a few minutes say:

Now repeat this conversation with body gestures and sound just like you did before, each taking a turn to speak without words We will share with words in a few minutes.

After a few more minutes say:

Pause.

Take a few minutes again to talk about how that felt in your body. Was it different from the "no?" Did you feel it in a different part of your body? Just notice what happened in your body and share with your partner.

Again, let's shake that off and let it go before we go on to the next step.

"Yes, And…"

Now we come to the last step and the fun part. Again, a good demonstration really helps. Many folks have not had much experience with "Yes, and…" from either side, but they will get the idea quickly. It is so joyful and energizing to respond this way and to get these responses that it has a built in motivation factor. Also, it is in tune with our basic nature and with the universal stream of well being, so it feels good to our bodies and our souls.

This language of the soul, communicated from my body to your body, sounds something like this:

"Yes, and I know some people who would like to help you with that."
"Yes, and I have a space you could use for free to try that out for a few weeks."
"Yes, and I am so appreciating the innovative thinking you are doing. You are so creative."
"Yes, and I would like to help in any way I can."
"Yes, and how do I sign up to participate?"
"Yes, and I know with your good planning skills, you will make this happen."

You can use these as ideas for your demo or remember your own.

We will take turns again presenting the same dream but this time the responder will be saying "yes, and…" I will call freeze when it is time to stop and switch roles. Don't forget to pause and let your partner respond.

OK, so here we go again.

After a much longer time say:

Pause.

Change roles now, giving your partner a chance to be affirmed. Begin.

After another generous time say:

Pause.

Now repeat this conversation with body gestures and sound just like you did before, each taking a turn to speak without words.

When that step is done, again say:

Pause.

Take a few minutes again to talk about how that was for you. Does having all that good support open you up to more love for yourself and your dreams? Take one last moment to appreciate each other however you wish for taking this journey to "yes" with you.

Walk out into the room moving and breathing and feeling that "yes" in your body and say "yes" to everybody you pass with gestures, words, facial expression, or just your body energy.

Facilitation Suggestions

Before doing this exercise with a group, I suggest that you prepare your participants with playful moving versions of saying "yes." Some examples of this are "Yes Let's" (above, p. 23), Connect the Dots" (p. 179) or "Seed" (p. 275 in the "Resources" section). Many more are available in my book *Dancing Our Way Home*, which contains hundreds of simple exercises for playing, creating, and connecting in community.

I usually have the musician speed up the music at the end and encourage the group to just "rock out" and celebrate the work they have done together.

I leave plenty of time in the "yes, and..." step, watching the group to see when they are complete. Partnerships have been born in this step.

(Many Thanks to S. Kate Moore.)

"Yes, And" Theatre

Here is one more fun and easy way to play and love yourself into the habit of "yes, and" as your answer to everything. This can be done with only two people or going around a circle with many participants.

One person begins a story, like a fairy tale or a myth, or using a dream, an incident from their day, or anything they want as the theme, and then they pause after a couple of sentences, and the next person moves the story forward and then pauses, and the story goes on until it comes back to the starting person. You just keep going around the circle or back and forth between two people like this for a few minutes until you are done with your story, until you can't quit laughing at your story, until you need to get a snack, or until someone calls time. And then you start a new story if you want. Your story can be serious or romantic or funny or outrageous, or make no sense at all. The idea is to have fun and to exercise the spontaneous "yes, and" part of your brain.

Here is one fairy-tale-like example of how it could go:

Person 1: Once upon a time there was a young girl who had a heart too big for her chest. She had to hide so the villagers wouldn't see her bulging chest and laugh at her. Pause.

Person 2: Yes, and every day she cried so much in her loneliness that a stream of water began to run out of her small hut on the edge of the village, and into the forest nearby. Pause.

Person 3: Yes, and little wild flowers and grasses began to bloom along the stream as it deepened into a wider and wider stream. The flowers filled the air with wonderful sweet fragrance. Pause.

Person 4: Yes, and one day, when she was so tired from all of her weeping she fell into a deep sleep. That day a soft wind came up and blew the sweet fragrance or the flowers into the little girl's hut, and she began to dream of a different life. Pause.

Person 5: Yes, and the smell of the flowers was so strong she rose up out of her bed and began to walk in her sleep into the forest, following the scent of the flowers and the sound of the little stream that was her tears.

And so forth…

Appreciations

Another very direct way to get to our "yes" is to look for what we can appreciate in the moment. The power of appreciating yourself, and everything and everybody around you cannot be overstated. Appreciations are simply the basic building blocks for a good life. Just increasing the number of appreciations we think and speak to ourselves and each other every day might be all the spiritual practice we would ever need to become a fully evolved human being.

I have even come to feeling a deep appreciation for my very violent and abusive father, as all of my life's work, all of my health with my loving children, all of my greater vision and deepest most meaningful parts of my life began with his violence and my response to it. Sometimes I am even inspired by myself, by how blessed and beautiful and amazing my life is! We are conditioned to expect and accept criticism and even consider ourselves evolved if we are good at receiving criticism. Our own very active inner critic is relentless and directs its energy toward others as well as toward ourselves. The solution is to add in appreciations as a conscious practice— creating a new habit and a new pattern of interacting with ourselves and with others. It is so exciting that we can do this, that our brain will do whatever we tell it to do!

Inspiring Appreciations

Here are some questions you could ask yourself to stimulate appreciations of yourself and your life:

What am I grateful for about the earth, the sky, the animals, the waters, the winds, the trees?

What am I grateful for about my family?

What am I grateful for about the country and the city where I live?

What do I appreciate about my essence, my core qualities?

What do I appreciate about my body, my brain, my health?

What do I appreciate about my energy?

What do I appreciate about my children, my partner, my friend, my house, my work?

What do I appreciate about my skills, my gifts, my knowledge?

What do I appreciate about my dreams?

What do I appreciate about my creativity?

What do I appreciate about the way I dress, the way I create my living space?

What do I appreciate about the ways I give and receive?

Here are some questions you could ask yourself to stimulate appreciations for others:

What do I appreciate about this person right in this moment?

What is particularly wonderful, amazing, or awesome about this person?

What is unique about this person's contribution to the world?

How does this person show up in my life, in community, in groups?

What strengths do I notice about this person?

How does this person help me or others?

What is unusual or interesting about how this person uses their creativity?

How has this person said yes to me?

What makes me happy when I am around this person?

How does this person give me attention?

What are ways this person always shows up?

What agreements does this person always keep?

What amazing things has this person already done in their life?

What have I learned from this person?

How has this person supported me in my journey?

How does this person manage change or challenges?

How does this person relate to spirit?

Here are some phrases to begin appreciation sentences:

I love the way I/ you…

I love how I / you…

I notice I/ you…

Thank you for…

I am grateful that…

I see my/ your…

I appreciate that you have…

I appreciate your…

I am amazed at…

I consistently see…

"Never Ending Gratitude"

This exercise, which is my personal favorite, is a fun and easy way to create a pattern of ongoing appreciations. I recommend starting each day with this game. It is guaranteed to make you smile and you can do it anywhere, any time. It lifts your spirits if they are down and reinforces your positive feelings in a heartbeat.

I do this every morning as I drive down the mountain from my house into town, or as I take my morning shower, or as I make my morning tea. (Eight appreciations before breakfast!) It is so fun to keep coming up with new ways to be grateful.

Everything that you are aware of around you and inside you and in your spiritual and energetic field is a miracle in your life and available for gratitude.

Begin speaking—stream of consciousness—about all the things you are grateful for in your life, all the ways you appreciate yourself, all the ways you appreciate nature, the clothes you are wearing, the clouds in the sky, your new shoes, your children and grandchildren, the fox you saw last night, your friends, your brain, your body, your health, your organs, the food you eat, the little bird singing outside you door, your heart, the house you live in, your neighbors, the post office, the grocery store full of food, the road you are driving on, the car you are driving, the little flower on the side of the road, the bus you are taking, etc. Just keep going until you are tired, run out of things to say for the moment, or arrive at your destination.

Inspired by Ester and Jerry Hicks.

Marking Your Appreciations
Another practice I did for myself for many years was to make a check on my calendar each time I appreciated myself

or somebody else. My agreement with myself was to have at least 30 marks a day, with the goal of creating a new way of viewing my life and those around me. If I got to the end of a day and noticed I had not remembered my appreciations that day, I got to do a whole bunch all at once to keep my agreement with myself. It is a great practice and really works.

I still check myself sometimes when I feel like I am slipping into old stories around not "being enough" or others not "being enough." The trick is to simply notice, and then correct my course, rather than making myself wrong or criticizing myself for not loving myself or others enough. To open the door to seeing and acknowledging others, I have to be seeing and loving myself, so it all blends together nicely.

If I am curious about why I forgot to appreciate myself that day, I can ask myself what needs some loving attention in me. Sometimes this is a simple matter of just loving my little girl who is tired and hungry, who just needs a break and a snack, and then she comes back to being positive and loving with herself.

Sometimes it is my "super competent self," who needs to be loved and appreciated for how much she got done that day. She will not relax and let me take good care of myself unless she gets appreciated for the gifts she brings. And if I love her enough, she relaxes into a very skilled and loving leader, who easefully keeps many balls in the air and loves doing it.

Sometimes it is not so simple, but love is still the answer. Many years ago now, I was going through a very rough time in my life. My father died, which had a greater impact on me than I expected, my brother was killed in an accident while riding his bike, and the man who was my husband decided to leave in the middle of all that and go to start a new life for himself.

I was not in charge of any of those events in any way. Nothing I did caused them to happen and there was nothing I could have done to prevent them. Yet, in my grief, I had slipped quietly back into old patterns of self-criticism. Without really being conscious of it, I had blamed myself in a general way, everything from feeling, "I should have spent more time with my brother while he was alive." to "If only I had been a better person, my husband wouldn't have left." I even felt bad that I was feeling so relieved to have my very abusive and very miserable father leave the earth—at 96 years of age!

Looking back, I can hardly believe that I took any responsibility for any of these events, and I get to love so deeply the little girl in me that was so oppressed, and that is such an enthusiast, such a striver, and that wants so much to be good and to do it right. She is a great asset when she is cared for and channeled through my loving mother energy. She provides great insights into what others are feeling, and she is filled with deep compassion for all living beings. She often guides me to my body wisdom and helps me remember that love, whether it is being sent in or out, is the baseline for healing and for an easeful joyful life.

It took the loving support of others who cared deeply about me, and several weeks of consistently appreciating and loving my little girl and my amazing woman self, to come out of the grief and self-criticism. Thinking about my brother-husband-father turned out to be one very interwoven story of "I am not enough." One incredible gift of the whole painful time was the letting go, on a much deeper level, of that story that "I am not ever enough, no matter how much I give or how hard I try." And that inner striver and survivor is also my gift—my achiever, my drive, my ability to make things happen— and now I know that I don't need to be relentlessly driven by that striver, and that I also very much appreciate her when I need her to help me complete or accomplish something.

Practicing saying "yes" to my children eventually shifted my relationship with myself, and I began to say "yes" to me. As I stepped more and more out of the role of victim, I was blessed with beautiful teachers and healers who helped me keep finding my way to an even deeper "yes," which sometimes meant making big changes in my life.

So we have come full circle back to where we began, with the story of loving our selves and saying "yes" to our selves so we can say "yes" to all of those around us.

And now we are ready to take a journey around the mandala through the healing cycle that I call "The Body Now."

"The Body Now"
Mandala

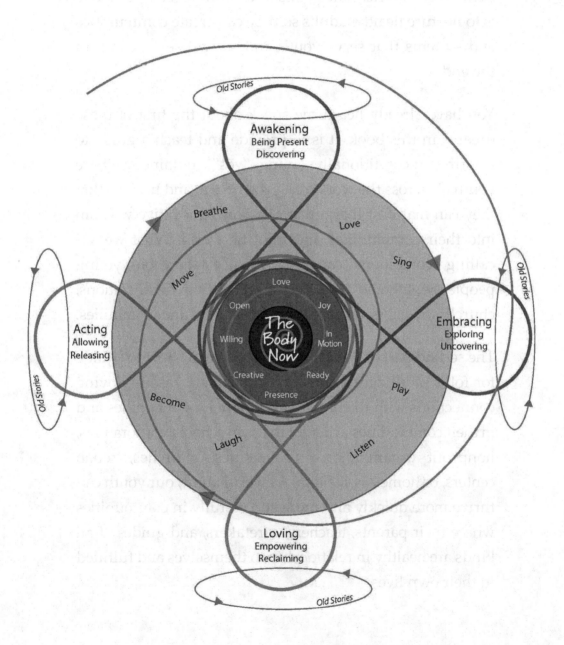

"The Body Now" Mandala

"The Body Now" healing cycle has evolved from living and breathing two dreams for over 30 years. The two dreams fold back on each other: one is to serve youth directly, and one is to nurture healthy adults so they can create communities and systems that serve youth and so will serve us all in the end.

You have already heard me speak about the first of these dreams in this book. It is to provide and teach a guide to creating unconditionally loving "yes" containers where youth all across the world can grow, learn, and heal, so that they can manifest their great gifts and innovative wisdom into their communities and into the world. What we are calling "containers" can be any place where our young people are gathered, including schools, youth organizations, churches, shelters, rehab centers, and all manner of families.

The second part of this objective is to offer a "how-to" guide for folks of all ages who want to facilitate easeful, loving connections with themselves and in their own families and in their communities, whether this is in schools, corporations, nonprofit organizations, universities, churches, rehab centers, or homeless shelters. As we all know, our youth can thrive more quickly and more successfully in communities where their parents, teachers, caretakers, and guides of all kinds are healthy in relationship to themselves and fulfilled in their own lives.

These two dreams move in a spiral together and reinforce each other over and over again. As we get healthier and move into a more positive, loving relationship with ourselves, we are able to be more generous and loving with those around us. They, in turn, respond more positively to us, and the norms of our community begin to change. Youth and adults alike show up differently as new expectations are modeled, and positive response and supportive energy become the norm.

A system where everybody is seen and has value paradoxically grows out of our willingness to see ourselves and our own value. This pattern grows quickly in the groups that Turning the Wheel facilitate, in part because it just feels really good to work and play and talk and risk and grow surrounded by positive, accepting energy.

So this model is addressing how we bring spirit and practice together and birth the "Yes" Collective everywhere we go. How do we find our way into our own bodies and then guide others there so we can all play together?

As we move through the model, the entry point will be very personal so you can come to your leadership with a clear vessel, ready to loop the loving acceptance you have for yourself to others. This begins with our awareness of our body knowing, and moves around "The Body Now" mandala through embracing to loving to acting. (See illustration p. 45.) When you are ready, you will also see suggestions for how to bring the personal visualization journeys to groups.

A wonderful teacher who came to our workshop ready to find positive, new ways to "manage" her students helped us articulate how the personal intersects with the group. She was working with a particularly challenged group of kids who came from experiences of violence and poverty. We suggested she put the whole story on the healing cycle and see if it changed for her.

I explained that whatever was going on in the room was partly a reflection back to us of what we were bringing to the room. This is often a tough concept for people to embrace. We are conditioned to believe that what is going on outside us is where the problem lies and where the change has to be made—the kids in our classroom, our children, our partners, our bosses, our work environment, or even the weather—are the real sources of the problem. The trouble is that we are not in charge of any of that. We are only in charge of ourselves and what we are bringing and how we are negotiating our own inner landscape of feelings and history and conditioning and physical sensations.

So we have a very different approach to how to "manage" our participants. If our facilitators are having a difficult time with a group, we suggest they take a moment and check in with themselves and see what is going on for them. Are they afraid they can't make the day work, feeling unprepared, actually afraid of the kids in the room, hungry because they didn't get breakfast, mad at their partner, overtired, worried about one of their own kids, or concerned about something else inside themselves?

The miracle is that once you tune into whatever that is, and get a snack or realize you can't do anything about your partner right now, or take a moment in the fresh air to breathe and refresh your energy, the room changes right before your eyes. As you settle into your body and embrace and attend to your own issues, they are pulled back off the people in the room. You put on a different lens as you look at that room, and it all changes instantly.

The kids do not look frightening anymore, and you are breathing now so you can access your creativity and make an immediate plan based on what is needed in the room, or you just see the whole group differently because you are not projecting your stress or stereotypical responses on them anymore. Regardless of what is going on for you, once you are aware of it and embrace its origin and love yourself just as you are, you will act differently and the participants will respond differently to you.

Our teacher called one day a few weeks later with such deep appreciation for the power of staying present with herself in all of her life, not just in the classroom. She said that not only was she reenergized and enjoying her teaching again, but that her relationship with her partner was transforming every day as she combined appreciations with this idea of taking responsibility for her own well-being.

So we begin a journey around "The Body Now" mandala with many visualizations and games and ideas for you to experience and pass along to others, all with the intent to support you on your path to falling in love with yourself and uncovering all of your genius and joyful, loving energy so you can be part of the spiral of healing and regeneration of yourself and of our youth and of the communities we all live in together.

Why Improvisational Movement?

You will see as we move through these exercises that they are based mostly in improvisational movement, where the gestures and impulses and movements come from following your body and seeing what wants to happen in each moment, moment by moment.

Life is really just one long series of improvisations. And improvising reflects your life in present time, where anything is possible, with complete permission to be yourself. As you begin to improvise, following your body into the space, you literally activate your preferences, curiosity, timing, senses, rhythms, pace, habits, stories, longings, feelings, creativity, and intelligence. This opens up new possibilities, revealing your particular contribution in each moment. Every one of these moments is the next incredible opportunity for life to unfold.

Just as we are reflected in nature, our bodies and our stories are reflected and played out in our spontaneous movement. All the skills we develop in improvisational movement integrate our ability to make choices about how we want to live our lives. Freeing up our movement, breath, and sound develops our ability to respond in the moment—activating our creativity and allowing us to live more fully in the endless joy of each moment.

Best of all, as we drop into our authentic movement, we also drop into an easeful, streaming feeling of well-being in the body that connects us to each other and the universe: the whole molecular, energetic, spacious, always-moving field.

As we relax into that stream of experience, we drop into the pool of deep knowing where creativity and discovery thrive. The creative act, the triumph of spontaneous new thought over habituated response, can elegantly prevail and can overcome every objection inside and outside of the creator!

And if that isn't enough, the most recent brain research indicates (perhaps not surprisingly) that spontaneous activity is the most effective way of keeping our brains healthy and alert, preventing Alzheimer's and other kinds of dementia as we age. So let's begin our journey through the healing cycle and see what happens moment to moment.

Moving through the Healing Cycle of "The Body Now" Mandala

Four Steps on "The Body Now" Mandala
I. Awakening, Being Present, Discovering
II. Embracing, Exploring, Uncovering
III. Loving, Empowering, Reclaiming
IV. Acting, Allowing, Releasing

This cycle, in its simplest form, is a movement-based journey to our essence that is an ongoing process of evolving with ease and love. Once you get started on the mandala, you just keep spiraling into more and more embodied joy. There is no beginning or end. You can enter at any point on the circle and have an immediate new beginning. The magic is in the willingness to make the first move, to actually step into well-being, into "being well." The brain will quickly rewire your system for this new choice and then keep rewiring as you continue to make new choices that move you deeper into your own authentic story.

The exciting thing about getting moving is that you can just spiral right to the middle of the "The Body Now" mandala, and you are home without doing any processing, changing your past, analyzing, suffering, or fixing yourself. Any time you really get moving and breathing, you will drop into your body, and the chemicals in your body that love you to move will start firing "feel-good" signals, and you will be back home to yourself. Add sounding and singing as you are moving, and the process is even quicker and more joyful.

If you are feeling stuck and waking up to your self is just not happening in this moment, there are lots of ways to get the energy moving again that are easy and fun. Take a look at the "Resources" section for ideas on ways you can keep moving, then add your own, and keep adding new ones every week. (See "Spiraling into The Body Now," p. 291.) As long as we are moving and breathing, we will find our way back to feeling good and to creating the moment we want, and then the next moment, each one building on the ease of the one before.

We organize our classes, gatherings, rituals, and trainings around a flow that always begins with a circle and ends with a circle. Just standing quietly and holding hands in a circle is, by itself, transforming for a community. All of our memories of connection, ancient and newly discovered, are activated, and participants settle in quickly. If you add in the idea of sending love around the circle through your hands, the whole energy in the room shifts.

In between, we move through "The Body Now" mandala (see p. 45), which moves from Awakening (Getting Present), to Embracing (Exploring), to Loving (Making Contact), to Acting (Connecting). In the arc of a class, this cycle translates correspondingly into "I am here," "You are here," "I see you," and "I see you and me together." If you are in a more individual exploration, it might be "I am here," "I see me," "I listen to me," and "I connect to myself."

Most of us go through this cycle many times in a day, maybe hundreds. Sometimes it takes a second and sometimes it takes an hour, but the sequence is the same: show up, see what is there, interact, and engage. So, let's begin with the first step, "Awakening."

Step I
Awakening "The Body Now"
Awakening, Being Present, Discovering

Affirmation: I am ready to awaken to the experience of me in my body.
I want to be in relationship to that which I am.

There is no more important relationship than the one with our own beloved self and all of its parts: strengths and weaknesses, desires and longings, and hopes and dreams.

Coming into relationship with our body is the beginning of coming home to that beloved self, to our authentic self. I believe that there is no healing, no transformation, no forward motion, and no sustainable change without a clear and moving relationship with the body.

Awakening to our bodies, listening to our bodies, and actually inhabiting our bodies, is the bridge to reclaiming our soul's journey, to remembering all that we have always known, and to retrieving all the parts of ourselves we have left behind along the way.

We left them behind for good reasons at the time—maybe in order to be safe, to be loved, to get approval, or to fit in. Now we get to reclaim these parts in order to experience our wholeness. This beautiful and exciting process of awakening to ourselves is the bridge to remembering what we have always known and who we were before someone else started writing our story. And connecting to our own deeper essence is the path to connection with all of life.

"The Body Now" mandala (p. 45), which grew out of my own journey back to my body, has been developed over the last 30 years of teaching and facilitating thousands people of all ages and backgrounds. It is simply the body in motion on the way home to its own true story, its own authentic journey. Wherever we enter the mandala and whatever path we take, we will land in "The Body Now" and solidly enter into our own breathing, moving, flowing, throbbing body, where everything is possible.

Getting Present

The first step on "The Body Now" mandala, "Awakening," is about getting present in the moment in our bodies. Really all of life is about getting present and then more present, embracing and following our bodies into living a life of authentically responding to each moment. We begin finding this presence by developing our own ability to witness ourselves, to notice sensations in our bodies, and to listen to the signals our bodies give us all the time.

Ask yourself: "What do I notice right now, in this moment, in my body?" Scan your body for sensations, or vibrations. Notice how and where in your body you are breathing right now. This choice to be curious about our body signals, and to consciously listen to our body, is the beginning of a lifelong practice, as the body is a dynamic, moving, energy field and is therefore always changing.

Tuning into the Body Cues

Try the simple exercise below to get a taste of how easy and fun it can be to notice your body cues and get moving (Awakening).

"Finding Sensation"

Take a few moments to stand with you feet hip-width apart and take some deep breaths. Scan your body for any sensation: in your muscles, your breath, your feelings, your bones, behind your eyes, in your fingers, your belly, your back. Then just lovingly notice that sensation.

Now just let your body move in response to that sensation easily and effortlessly. Let your thinking and self-consciousness rest for a moment and just let your body lead, following the sensation you found in your body.

What does this sensation want to do, how does this sensation move if it is leading, does it have a sound that it wants to express?

Is this sensation changing or moving to another place in your body? Is it intensifying, asking for more attention?

Keep moving until you feel a shift in your body that lets you know you are in an easeful place in your body.

Then just take a moment to appreciate yourself for your awareness and your willingness to move and breathe yourself into well-being.

Facilitation Suggestions

If you are leading a group and have participants who can't find any sensation in their body to get started with, have them create a sensation to start moving from. They might make a fist, or tighten their jaw, or smile, or flex one foot, and then begin moving from there.

"Shining the Light"

Here is another simple yet very powerful way to stay curious about your own body story. This process can be done every day for the rest of your life and it will always bring new awareness. I have incorporated it into my evening meditation.

Close your eyes and turn on your inner lights and shine the light of love unconditionally into all the "nooks and crannies" of your body, opening up to seeing all of you. Stay with this awhile, shining this warm loving light all through the interior of your body. Notice places that seem to have been in darkness and give them a little more time in the warm, loving light.

Now allow yourself to feel curious about what is going on in your body. You might ask yourself: What am I experiencing in my body right now? Maybe you are noticing that your tummy is growling, your knees are hurting, or your heart is racing. Maybe your arms feel a little shaky, your neck is feeling stiff, the bottoms of your feet are tingling, or you feel hungry or tired or have lots of energy moving around in your body.

Just notice and then love what you are seeing just the way it is— saying "yes" to all that is present in that moment in your actual body sensations. Send some loving attention to a sensation that is calling to you, maybe surrounding that place with some warm, soothing light. Changing something always comes after loving it the way it is and appreciating and trusting the body wisdom of that moment.

Here is a variation on this exercise that can provide another way to access sensation. You can also weave it into the end of the exercise above.

Scan your body for a place that you particularly like (or love) right now. Move from that place and let it have some sound or rhythm if it wants to. Find another place that you are happy about and that wants to play. Maybe notice a place you are turning away from in your body and invite that place to come and play too. Let your body lead and have fun discovering where it takes you.

What happens when we illuminate our inner landscape is truly the stuff of magic. Magic is, after all, simply enhanced focus, and focus on our own body—our blood, our breath, our fluids, our bones—is the beginning of the end of suffering in our lives.

Now take a moment and truly appreciate yourself for being conscious of your body speaking to you and for being willing to notice what your body is telling you. Our bodies will always tell us the truth about ourselves (and others), if we listen.

This was certainly not what most of us were taught as children. I have really clear memories of saying something as simple "I'm hungry," and the response being "No you're not. You just ate." "I'm cold." "You're not cold. It's warm in here." "I'm tired of doing this. You aren't tired, you just got started." I'm sure you can add examples that you remember and that you still say to yourself today.

As an adult, that childhood voice can become an active inner voice, which argues with our own body reality: "I have had enough to eat." or "What is the matter with me? I just ate." or "I don't know why I am cold all the time these days." Or "I don't need to turn the heat up, it is not that cold in here," and on and on.

Moment by Moment, Body to My Body

The most direct pathway to living more consistently in a state of peacefulness is to become more aware of your body signals, to listen to them, and then make choices based on what your body is telling you. If what you are doing, thinking, or imagining feels good, then you are on the right track. If your body is giving you a "no" in any form, then head another direction, towards the "yes."

You can choose to drop into your body in any moment by simply taking a deep breath and moving in any way you want, little or big. Moving and breathing will do it all, especially if you pause long enough to drop all the way in. It is not possible to stay closed and move.

Moving the body opens your heart and helps you grow in your capacity for feeling ease and flow. If you move and breathe yourself into presence in your body and then witness yourself with love, you will be making a conscious choice that will nurture your higher self and all of those around you too.

It is so simple we don't even see it as revolutionary, and that is the good news! We already know everything we need to know to have the life we want. We just need to illuminate that information for ourselves, shine that loving light of awareness into every part of our beings—physical, energetic, and spiritual bodies—and then celebrate and honor the depth and power of that knowing.

The more awareness we have of our own incredible body and its signals, the more we will appreciate and love that body: one of the most amazing, mysterious, ancient, and outrageously intelligent organisms we know. The more we truly love and appreciate all of our being, the more room we have in our hearts to love others, all others. And what we have developed in "The Body Now" model provides many different effective and well-demonstrated ways to get to that place of giving and receiving love with ease.

Entering the Magic of Our Fluids
I feel my fluids resonating with the ancient songs of unity and divine love.

In all of my journeys over the last 50 years to open the channels of the body-mind connection, nothing has been as powerful or as available as dropping deeply into the fluid system of my body. Moving with the fluids of your body is a very gentle way to reclaim your own soul's journey and find your way back to the story that belongs only to you, to your deep knowing through the freeing of the fluids. Vibrating with all the fluids of the earth allows our bodies to integrate and to all weave together into one huge web of watery, moving, ancient wisdom.

Your body is nourished and healed over and over by the movement of fluids within your cells and tissues, fluids that are bathing your body in unconditional love and ease and well-being all the time. The most direct way to health and well-being that I know of is to keep that flow going, to release any still or frozen spots where the fluids are not moving and then relax into the magical, nurturing energy of the moving fluids.

All stress ultimately can be measured by the flow of the fluids in our bodies. Fluids move through our bones, our brains, our cells, our veins, and our hearts, creating connections inside and outside our bodies all the time.

"Fluid Journey—Water Dreaming"

The following journey is a gentle and deeply nourishing way to awaken to your fluid body. An audio recording available online (www.turningthewheel.org/audio) will guide you through a solo version of this exercise. Try doing this a few times for yourself before using the script below to guide a group through this journey.

Beautiful flowing music is so helpful here. We resonate so quickly with music, and participants can often drop right into this exploration if the music is in alignment with the fluids.

Begin walking in the room and just release into your natural breath and rhythm of this moment, letting your awareness begin to float down around your body, as you gently come into your body, letting all the pieces of you come home. Feel them dropping down into your core and breathe them gently in. Maybe your eyes are toward the floor; your jaw and belly are relaxed.

Slowly begin to play with releasing your muscle structure and your bones and be like a Raggedy Ann doll, floppy and free. Allow everything in your body to let go into the fluids: fluid fingertips, fluid behind your eyes and between your ears, fluid spine and neck. Let your head float on top, released from the restrictions of the neck.

Pause.

Now imagine you are dropping down into the water and feel yourself floating in the warm water, carried and held in the buoyancy of the water. Let your whole body release into the warm support of the water.

Try moving as if you are floating in that warm watery womb, moving freely and effortlessly. Your arms and legs are floating up through the water; your spine and neck are released and relaxed. There is no contraction in your body, just floating free, all released. Notice the patterns in the water and the reflections of the light, mirroring your body state.

Pause.

Try becoming the water, flowing over the earth feeling the swirling currents in the flow and the way the water seeks the easiest route, flowing in and out…, over and under…, around and through…. Notice the relationships the water forms with the pathways it spontaneously chooses.

Let all of the contraction and compression in your body flow into the watery you, moving effortlessly and joyously through the room, a luminous fluid body.

Find a partner and be fluids together, moving and playing together, interacting from that flowing, easy, watery place. You might be responding to each other or leading and following each other or just frolicking through the room, letting the freedom of your "fluidy" body guide you.

Slowly make your way back into the circle, bringing all that joy with you.

Facilitation Suggestions

To close this exercise, I often lead a watery "Copy Circle" (p. 262) and then sing a simple community song together, like "I Was on the Rolling Sea" (www.turningthewheel.org/songs).

Be sure to pause in between the paragraphs and watch your group, taking your timing from what you see in the room and what you feel in your body, looping out to the group and then looping back in to yourself.

Good Attention

Another way to step into awareness on the healing cycle is to give yourself some loving attention and then loop that out to someone else. Attention is innately healing and can create new patterns, restore balance to our lives, and bring unknown or unclaimed potentials into manifestation. We actually cannot live without attention, and one really important source of that attention is our own appreciation of ourselves. Creating the life we long for is like creating art, only now we are painting and dancing our dreams into existence. If you turn all of your good attention toward loving a part of yourself that you want more of, it will happily show up.

Unfortunately, very few of us have had enough positive attention. And certainly most of the youth we work with have had almost none in their lives at all. Because you are part of this western culture, you have probably internalized a deep resistance to either giving yourself good attention or to receiving it from others. You don't want to be seen as a "show-off" or as "high maintenance." And even worse, what if you wanted too much attention or you were taking up all the attention in the room. How many times in your life were you told to settle down or to be quiet?

Making the choice to turn consciously toward acknowledging and appreciating yourself is the next step after you have activated your fluids. They will carry this message of loving self throughout your whole body easily and happily. All of our life experiences begin with our choices, and they are sustained by those choices and ultimately ended by those choices.

We get to choose whether we will make those choices from a place of consciousness, or by default, governed by old stories. The body-mind connection, which some considered ludicrous not too long ago, is now widely accepted. We know we have neurological connectors that carry our feelings directly to our cells. (See the discussion of "peptides," on p. 209.) Your body reflects and lives into what you are feeling.

This next exercise is a truly transforming step into giving yourself this loving attention. You can do this journey one time or every day for a week if you love it and want to anchor it firmly in your body. I use this exercise to restore myself if I have dropped into old stories of not being good enough or wishing I were different than I am. Every time I do this, I am delighted and surprised to uncover new pieces of myself that want to be seen and loved. The audio of this exercise (www. turningthe wheel.org/audio) will allow you to drop easily into the process and just enjoy the journey. You can then use the script below to bring this gift to a group.

"Walking the Path of Self Love"

Begin walking in the room, breathing and making whatever sounds your body wants to make: sighing, deep toning, high wailing, joyful tones, soft sounds, staccato sounds, sustained tones, etc.

Take this time to arrive in the room and feel your body presence, checking in with your body sensations. You may want to a scan your body for a moment and see if any place needs a little attention or release or celebration.

Just keep moving and breathing, and dropping into your fluids, until you feel like you are here. Then just pause and drop into your feet, and say quietly and slowly to yourself a few times, "I am here." "I am here."

Starting from this place where you have paused, we are going to walk the path of self-love, letting your body lead you through the room.

As you are walking, review all the ways you have been incredible, amazing, kind, generous, and breathtaking in the last ten years— times you showed up for somebody else, times you showed up for yourself, times you appreciated someone at just the right time, times you made something happen that you wanted to see happen, times you gave fully of yourself to someone else, times you gave fully to yourself.

Pause many times along the way and acknowledge those memories, letting your incredible, amazing self be honored and seen by you.

Pause.

Do a little love dance, or movement celebration, for yourself at each pause, and maybe some singing and sounding too. See what wants to happen in your body, just letting it rise up.

Remember that the ancestors are always there with you watching your magnificence, dancing your joy, and singing you songs. Feel those dances in your bones, and listen for those songs. Let them come through your body as you are moving down your path of self-love.

Pause.

Move your love story to yourself, caressing and playing and flowing down the path. Let those ancient sounds that love you and nurture you come through your throat, singing a love song to yourself.

Pause.

Drop into your fluids, and let this loving awareness circulate through your whole body, bathing your essence in the sound and movements of breathtaking love.

Open up your essence to the waters of the earth that are ancient and all knowing, always moving and changing and evolving, and let that infinite source of well-being flow right into your fluid body and bathe you in loving kindness.

Pause.

Continue on your path praising yourself and your ancestors and your guides and connections to source—moving and singing and sounding your gratitude to the stream of well-being that shines so much love on you and the waters that rock you in their endless wisdom.

As you begin to come back into the room, let your hands begin to touch your body and feel the boundaries of your body, the way your skin holds you all together, and the muscles and bones that live within the fluids. Notice the breathtaking way your body serves you and guides you in your life, just taking a moment to appreciate the magic and mystery of your amazing being.

Facilitation Suggestions

I deliver the text for this exercise slowly, pausing a lot between ideas, reflecting the pace of the room.

Bring all of the participants together in a circle holding hands and close with a song like "Knowing Love" (www. turningthewheel.org/songs) or with sounding together or just standing together in silence.

After a few moments have the participants blink their eyes open and see each other, thanking each other with their eyes for the beautiful folks who have shown up to journey into consciousness together.

Then just have them turn towards a partner to share how that experience was for them, giving them time to check in and reenter the present time. While they are with this partner would be a good time for them to each share an appreciation of themselves.

Old Stories

Sometimes we uncover some old stories when we enter a journey of self-love like the one above. Because the "Yes" Collective is all about moving into the next moment and the next, we are particularly interested in letting go of any places we are stopped by these old scripts. It is only in stillness that we begin to contract around old beliefs. Once we are moving again, and our fluids are flowing again, our creativity is restored, and we head back into our authentic self and our authentic life.

Hovering nearby on each step of "The Body Now" mandala are the "Old Stories" that spin around in our psyche. They are always willing to show up again and teach us their lessons again, perhaps on a deeper level each time. (See the illustration on p. 45.) The trick is to not get stuck in them, but to put them right on the healing cycle and keep them moving.

I spoke a few weeks ago with a woman I was working with who had recently left her husband and was making good progress on her path towards giving herself permission to be happy and to have what she wanted in her new space and in her new life.

She had an interaction with her husband that triggered her old beliefs around needing to meet the needs and demands of others in order to be lovable. Within seconds—really nanoseconds (one nanosecond is to one second as one second is to 31.71 years)—she was deep into self-criticism and certain that she was a selfish, uncaring person. She had inherited this story, or belief, from her mother.

The exciting thing for me to witness was how quickly she put the whole interaction on "The Body Now" healing cycle and circled through to a place of feeling good. She had noticed the contraction and stillness in her body when the criticism came at her (Awakening) and decided to make a different choice this time.

Instead of defending herself or withdrawing into silence (the old story), she began to move and breathe and scan her body for places that needed some attention (Awakening). She noticed that she felt a little nauseous, and that her throat was really tight and scratchy. As she stayed with her exploration she felt a shakiness inside her body, a "quivering all over deep inside, like my cells are shaking."

It seemed possible that she was still carrying that "unlovable story" deep in the tissues of her body (Embracing). Instead of making that wrong, she turned towards the part of her, her little girl, that was frightened, and picked her up and talked to her and loved her and reassured her that it was fine for her to want things for herself and that she would help her get them and take care of her (Embracing and Loving).

Then she called a friend to get the support she needed to stay committed to loving and nurturing herself (Acting). Within 15 minutes she had restored herself to a feeling of well-being and moved back into her day (Releasing). It was a beautiful example of putting something on the healing cycle and coming right back into alignment with yourself, moving back into the present moment.

As the old stories move themselves out of the forefront, because you have consciously asked them to, space opens up in your body, in your psyche, and in the fields surrounding you. New ideas, activities, relationships, and possibilities can come into that space. Everything starts moving with you and you feel the ease and joy in your life return. Your awakening turns into discovering the parts of you that have been waiting to get some good attention and they come out to play with you.

A fast route to choices that don't serve us is the cultural default story that life is supposed to be hard, that we are supposed to suffer. My dear friend Diana's Grandma used to call this "Lose a few, Lose a few." My mother's version of giving up was, "Well, you live till you die." And my version was, "I can do this, no matter what," which was maybe better than giving up completely but was still a guaranteed path to stress and martyrdom.

In TTW, the young people we work and create with often are carrying a deeply ingrained belief of hopelessness. They live in a culture that absolutely agrees that they will never have anything they want and often defines them as "losers." And they often live in communities that are trapped in deep cultural patterns of oppression, violence, and poverty.

Luckily we all have other parts of ourselves that know better: parts that know we are here to wake up every morning in joy, to live each day in ease, and to do work that feels like play to us. And the work we do with these young people around discovering their own value and appreciating their gifts can take them back into that "knowing." Love will always trump the old story—no matter how grim the story, or how committed we are to it.

Years ago we worked with an amazing young man I will call Michael, who came to us from the court system with an electronic bracelet and a "tracker," a supervisor he had to get permission from to do anything except go to school and go home. Home was a sketchy place at best, and violent at worst, so he was really anxious to get permission to join us for a full-scale production in the local theatre that would require three weeks of commitment from him, including some time during school hours and after school until 9 pm each evening.

He would be building sets, assisting with costumes and an audio installation, and learning the very complex set of cues for the hour-long performance so he could perform with us. We worked with the tracker, who warned us repeatedly against trying to engage with this young man who was "on his last chance to stay out of lockdown," but eventually we convinced him to give Michael permission to join us.

None of us had anything to say when Michael went outside to smoke on his breaks (on his last birthday his present from his mother was two cartons of cigarettes), or when he withdrew occasionally the first couple of days into silent depressions, or when he didn't respond to a request. Instead, every time he did respond, every time he showed up ready to work, and every time he ate healthy food with us, helped one of the cast learn their part, played games with the kids in the cast when they were restless, helped our elder walk down the stairs, offered a great creative solution to how to install a part of the set, or laughed out loud, we noticed and appreciated him, helping him shine the light on parts of himself that were not being seen anymore and maybe had never been seen. We really liked this kid. His intelligence, creativity, and kindness made our job easier, and we felt grateful to have his help.

The tracker had stayed away except to pick Michael up each evening at 9 pm on the dot. We were so involved in getting our show up we didn't pay much attention to him except to say hello. One evening he came early and watched our preparations for rehearsal and the first part of our rehearsal that evening. He was shocked at the way Michael was working with us, swore he had never seen that side of him, and wanted to know "What in the hell we were doing with him?" He was actually angry that Michael was acting differently for us than he did for him, with seemingly no awareness of the difference in how we talked to him or the way we viewed him. We didn't try to change the tracker, he hadn't signed up for that, so we just looped him some love and friendliness, and kept our focus on Michael.

Michael experienced people speaking kindly to each other and creating in the moment while working peacefully together. He got a taste of his competence, his intelligence, and his ability to be a part of a team. Most of all, he experienced what it felt like to show up as himself, his innately caring and joyful self, and to have an impact and make a difference for others. Michael learned that you don't have to change the past to create a new future.

"Going toward the Open Space— A Journey to Ease and Joy"

We are here because we are all becoming, we are evolving, and we are loved and held in that evolution. If we let the love flow through us and add our conscious intentions, it can be easy and effortless to keep moving forward. It is trying to stop our evolution that creates suffering in our lives.

Moving into the open spaces that are free of old stories and that are there for you, both in your psyche and in your physical body, can become one of your positive, new default positions. Once you have done this exercise a few times, and maybe in a few different ways, you may start to notice when you are going toward the open space in your life and when you are headed down into struggle. You will feel a contraction in your body. Once you notice the contraction, you can change course and head back out into the open space, a quick and easy reset.

Find a quiet space for the next twenty minutes and try this exercise with a group of friends. You can do it alone using the audio recording (www.turningthewheel.org/audio), which is created for one person to experience. The script below is written for a group. Like many such journeys, this exercise will be richer when done with a group. You feel the energy and support from each other as you go, and you can interact with others when that is part of the directions. Then you can share with each other at the end, which is always an invaluable part of the exercise.

Begin by just walking and breathing and moving in the room, seeing others around you but just resting your focus internally.

Notice what you are saying to your brain right now? What you are telling yourself, right now? Just notice and keep walking. Add in moving your arms as you walk—any way you wish.

Try telling your brain what you want right now and see how that feels. Speak out loud to your brain if you wish, kind of like praying out loud. What would you like to say to your brain—to yourself? Just notice what comes up for you and love and appreciate it all.

Now add in movement in your torso and legs as you are walking— anything that your body wants—gestures, wiggles, side steps and backward steps, turns, undulations, shaking…. Keep moving and come back into your breath, then see what you are telling yourself now. Is your message changing as you give yourself attention? Again, just notice—without any judgment—just moving and breathing and listening to yourself.

As you relax into your body, turn toward an open space in your body is in this moment. Where does there seem to be some room to breathe and shift? Move gently into that space, exploring the ease and comfort of moving toward the openness and hanging out there.

Follow this open space and see where it takes you internally. Let your body lead you around from opening to opening.

Where does this openness in your body take you in the room? Let your whole being open to awakening without agenda to the moment you are in. Live into the impulse for harmony, and just show up in the ease of this moment.

Take a moment in this easy, open space and scan your body for a place that feels good. Focus on that place, give it attention, let it move, and see if it has any sound to express.

Find another place that feels good. Give that place some attention too and let the two of them dance together and expand together. Find another place and invite that place into the dance. Notice the good feelings spreading and growing as you keep giving attention to what feels good. Have fun playing and dancing with all these parts that feel good and want to come out and play.

Interact with others in the group if you wish, letting your moving, happy essence stream through you and play with their "feeling-good" energy.

Keep moving and let go of all instructions and listen to your body. What does your body want right now? What wants to happen in this moment… and in this moment…and in this moment? How does your energy want to interact with others in the room? Just notice: moment to moment, body to body.

For the next 10 minutes, explore your own energy and impulses from one moment to the next. Sound is fine, too. You may be moving very slowly or very quickly, alone or with others. This is your time to follow your own body signals. What wants to spontaneously emerge from you right now?

Facilitation Suggestions

As your group is finishing, quietly bring them together in a circle by putting your hands out and inviting them in. They will form up slowly and easily and then you can close with a "Copy Circle" (p. 262 in the "Resources" section) or some sounding or singing together.

Live music or your own fun and upbeat recorded music is great for the end of this exercise.

A "Sounding Circle" (p. 281 in the "Resources" section) works really well after this exploration. Sound really does open up spaces and is a great way for some participants to land more completely in their bodies.

Or you can just use the short script below to guide your group into a gentle moment of sounding into their bodies. If you have taught the signature sound (see p. 106) to your group, you could just have them come back to their hum.

Begin humming your hum and let the sound drop all the way through your body, down through your organs, all the way down to your toes and back up again to the top of your head. Just let the sound circulate through your body.

As we close together, send your hum around the circle and feel the blend of our songs for this moment.

Morning Practices

Starting your day creating open space is a wonderful way to set up your day for success. How we begin the day is such a big part of how the day unfolds. If we begin by getting present in our bodies and coming into our awareness of all that is good in our lives and all the blessings of our life, everything follows from there.

The following practices are a few of my favorites, all fun and easy ways to drop into our gratitude and joy. All of these and many other ideas for "Morning Practices" are gathered in one place for you in the "Resources" section beginning on page 305.

"Never Ending Gratitude"

Everything that you are aware of around you and inside you and in your spiritual and energetic field is a miracle in your life, and available for gratitude. This exercise, described in detail on p. 305, is my personal favorite way to begin my day. It is guaranteed to make you smile and you can do it anywhere, any time.

"Body Sensations"

This is the beginning of awakening to our bodies, which we also visited at the very beginning of this chapter. It is a great way to start the day. It is also a great place to return to if you are feeling disconnected or confused. Sensation pathways are a very reliable way to get back into your body, and you can easily coach yourself.

Scan your body for a place that feels good, focus on that place, give it attention, let it move, and see if it has any sound to express. Find another place the feels good. Let the two of them dance together; expand together.

Let the good feelings expand and grow as you keep seeking sensations that feel good and keep bringing them into your dance. Have fun just inviting your moving, happy, essence stream you and around the room.

Notice how the positive energy spreads and grows as you keep giving attention to what feels good.

"Out Loud Praise for the Earth and for Yourself"

This is a very old and basic shamanistic practice that is common in slightly different variations in many different cultures and tribal groups. The shaman or spiritual guide of the tribe begins the day with a song of praise for the ancestors, the earth, and all the spirit beings that guide life. In some groups the whole community does this together in a ritual form they all are familiar with.

Either way, it is a powerful way to ground yourself in gratitude as you begin your day, remembering all that is there to hold you and support you. I like to take it one more step and think of myself as a member of a tribe and praise myself for what I will bring to my tribe, as the day unfolds.

Go out on your deck or in your front yard or stand where you can look out the window, or imagine a window for yourself looking at whatever pleases you and, speaking out loud, begin to praise the earth in every way you can think of, from the flowers that you see in your garden to the piles of snow in your driveway, to the trees in the park nearby.

Praise what you can't see in the moment also, like the high mountains or the rhythms of the ocean waves, or wild meadows filled with fragrant yellow flowers.

Praise your ancestors and thank them for your life here on the beautiful earth.

Finally, praise yourself for the love and service you will bring to the earth this day.

When you feel complete, you can continue on with "Never Ending Gratitude" (see p. 305) or write the "Song of Praise" described below if you have a little more time.

"A Song of Praise"

The more we use all of our different modes of expression, like moving, writing, painting, drawing, dancing, singing, listening, smelling, and even just opening our eyes to new dimensions, the more engaged and excited our brain gets.

The writing exercise described below is another way to express praise that you can do every morning in your journal if you wish. A series of "sentence stem" prompts offers starting points for writing your own "Song of Praise." I have written at least 200 different praise songs over the last 12 years and still find them very satisfying and helpful when I want to tune into loving myself or need to reset my heart and soul.

I have included a sample of one I wrote with the prompts highlighted in case it is helpful, but there is no right or wrong way to do this. There are worksheet versions of the "sentence stem" prompts for male writers and for female writers as well as one that is gender neutral. You can find these on p. 314 in the "Resource" section. You can make copies of the one you want to use and copy some of the others if you are working with a group so they can choose which one they want to use.

When you are ready, find a quiet place to begin writing. As you are writing, keep changing your position as described below. If you want to stop at a certain time, be sure to set a timer so you can really drop all the way into the exercise and not worry about watching the time.

We will write for about 20 minutes. If you are doing this exercise on your own, set a gentle sounding timer so you will know when to stop. Just fill in the sentence stems with your own answers. You could spend your whole time writing any one of these sentence stems or answer them all with only a few words or skip any that do not resonate for you. This is your "Song of Praise," and you are in charge of how you want to manifest it.

Begin writing when you are ready, and as you are writing, keep changing your position a little or a lot. You could write lying on your back or belly or walking around the room or with your paper up on the wall. Or you could just uncross your legs or change the direction you are facing. I will remind you to change your body position a couple of times in the next 20 minutes.

Let's begin together. Close you eyes for a moment and notice any places in your body that need to release or relax a little, and send those places some warm, loving energy and support.

Now move around a little and take a deep breath and wiggle a little until you feel present. Begin writing as you are ready.

Facilitation Suggestions

If you wish to guide a group through this exercise, you may want to add an opportunity for sharing at the end of the script above. When we take the connections that we have made to ourselves and share them with others, we embrace our insights more fully. This process of revealing ourselves is the ground for all real connection with others, connection that opens our hearts, deepens our knowing, and enriches our lives.

A Sample Song of Praise

My name is Alana. **I am the daughter of** Helen Leora, **the granddaughter** of Ruby Kincaid, and the **great-grand daughter of** Lena Browning. I am the Mother of Matthew, Andrea, Cassandra, Norah, Lucas, Aaron, and Morgan. I am the grandmother of Tobias, Jayda, Lila, Elias, Benjamin, Margaret, Caitlin, and Sage.

I sing my love and gratitude to the earth: to the waters, to the trees, to the birds and the winds, to the warmth of the sun and the wisdom of the moon.

I sound my deep spirit story and send blessings to my children and their children as they stand in their truth and reach for new ways to live and love together.

I thank my body for giving me health and serving me in my work, bringing me lots of good energy, and strength.

I praise my essence, which guides me in tenderness to manifest my authentic self and live my own soul's journey.

I praise my beating heart and send love to all the children of the earth.

I praise my unique contribution, which I will happily bring to everyone who wants to dance and laugh and play and live in joy with me.

I call in my Spirit Guides today, and ask, with gratitude, for guidance around stepping more fully and courageously into my self, and showing up 100% in every moment.

"Name Dance"

This exercise is another fun way to use writing to activate your curiosity, access some new ways of seeing yourself, and maybe find a little of your inner poet. Making the movement phrase at the end is easy and often surprising for the creator. I love that it reminds us that we are all dancers and creators—whether in the flow of our daily lives or the flow of our gestures.

You can do this on your own using the audio recording (www.turningthewheel.org/audio) when you get to the part where you make the movement phrase. However, making the movement phrase in a group is really fun. You get to witness all the different amazing authentic phrases that people make and have the wonderful experience of feeling your admiration and appreciation for each one.

You also get to be witnessed and seen by others in your creative energy, and that is a powerful agent of change for many folks. I often have the group share what they particularly liked about what they saw after each little performance, and it is amazing how much that can reinforce and enrich the participants' creative gifts.

The script below is for leading a group through the whole process. Reading it through will be helpful to you even if you are doing the exercise on your own.

Have your participants get their pen, find the "Name Dance" sheet on page 275 in the "Resources" section at the end of this book, and find a spot to settle into for writing. Remind them of all the ways they can shift their positions for maximum creativity while writing, and that they can make this exercise fit their own needs in this moment.

If you get stuck, try walking around the room while you write, or lying on your back, or shifting how you are sitting, the direction you are facing, or writing about how stuck you feel. Your perspective and creativity will shift if you shift your body—a wonderful guaranteed quick fix when you want to keep moving forward.

You can also skip back and forth between the questions as thoughts occur to you, write any thoughts that occur to you even if they don't seem to be answering the question, and skip questions entirely if they don't call to you. We will spend about 20 minutes doing this exercise.

Facilitation Suggestions

When the participants are finished, have them share with a small group or a partner, remembering that taking the time for this really deepens the learning and the friendships in your group. This writing can bring up past stories for some participants, so I usually circulate through the groups and check in to be sure everybody is doing OK.

Making the Movement Phrase

Now you can use this writing as the basis for creating a movement phrase all together, which is a great way to play together and embody the experience at the same time.

Take a moment and read over what you have written.

Let a word that you just really love pop out and circle it.

Now find a word that you feel curious about and circle it.

Find a word that brings up the future for you and circle it.

Last one: find a word that needs some loving attention and circle it.

Bring your paper to the circle and put it on the floor in front of you so you can refer to it if you need to.

Now you are ready to begin to make movements for each of these words, using them as inspiration. You are not trying to make a movement that people could guess the meaning of, like charades or mime. However, you do want your movement to have meaning and intention for you. You can see why you took that shape or moved in that way, and you could tell us about that choice.

Get your first word in your mind, the one you loved, and when I say, "1, 2, 3, GO" make a shape for that word, whatever your body does in the moment.

Let's do that one more time. When I say "1, 2, 3, GO," see what your body does this time. You might surprise yourself.

Beautiful. Choose the one of those you like the best and repeat it a few times so your body will remember it.

Now get your second word in your mind, the one you feel curious about, and take a few moments on your own time to explore some different gestures or shapes for this word.

Then pick the one you like the best and again repeat that movement so your body will remember it.

These are incredible. Now, let's put those two movements or shapes together. They make the beginning of your movement phrase.

Ready......, movement one, movement two.
Again........, movement one, movement two.

That looked amazing, so authentic and immediate. Now take your third word, the one that takes you forward into the future and turn to a partner near you and share with them what this word means to you.

Now turn your back to the circle so you are facing out of the circle and make a gesture for this word when I say, "1, 2, 3, GO."

Let's do that again, making another shape for this same word. "Ready, go." And one more. "Ready, go."

Good. Now choose the one you like the best of those again, and add it to your movement phrase, putting all three movements together. Repeat them a few times so you can do them without having to think too hard.

Come back to the circle and take your last word, the one that needs loving attention, and trade it with the partner that you were just sharing with. So you will have your partner's word and he or she will have your word. Now you are connecting in community, revealing to each other, and being allies for each other.

Holding your partner's word in your heart, begin to walk through the room shining a light of love on this part of your partner that needs some attention. Notice where you are responding in your body and move the way your body wants to move in response to these feelings.

Notice what movement or movements feel particularly in alignment for you and repeat them a few times so you can remember them and then add them to your dance. Take a moment and add this movement to your other three gestures to complete your movement phrase for now.

When you are complete, practice the four movements of your phrase several times so you get it in your body. Let's go through them together again. Movement one, movement two, movement three, movement four. One more time. Movement one, movement two, movement three, movement four. These are outrageously beautiful. I want you to be able to see what I am seeing.

There is one final step you can do before we share if you wish. Now that you know your phrase you can play a little bit with the connecting points of the movements, the transitions between them. Do you want to make it really smooth, really jerky, really slow, or really fast? What do you like best for your dance? For example, you might connect the first and the second with a percussive transition and then the second and third really slowly.

Practice your dance with the transitions integrated. You now have a beautiful dance phrase based on your own story in this moment. Find a partner and show them your movement phrase. Be sure to share with your partner what you particularly liked or enjoyed about their dance.

Facilitation Suggestions

I end this by having everyone come back to the circle and show their dances in groups of three, with each person going two times through their dance and then holding their last shape. This way everyone gets to be seen, and everyone gets to see and appreciate the incredible originality and impact of these beautiful little pieces. It is important to take a moment to appreciate these dances out loud and let the group say what they particularly liked in each group of three.

This is a great exercise to mix into day-long or weekend workshops. It lets your participants discover new ways of exploring themselves, creates new brain connections for some, and for others lets them hang out in places they may be more comfortable, like writing.

For other ideas to vary your ways of stepping into self-love, check out the art projects on page 232 in the "Resources" section at the end of this book, which can easily be integrated into your teaching symbolically. Possibilities include writing a love postcard to yourself and decorating the front, creating a treasure box to protect or honor the magic pieces of yourself, or making a magic wand of empowerment.

Step II
Embracing "The Body Now"
Embracing, Exploring, Uncovering

Affirmation: I am ready to embrace my awareness of my body and deepen into my journey of uncovering.

"Embracing" is taking all the energy you generated by waking up and witnessing yourself at the start of the mandala and using it to uncover the new and wonderful parts of yourself that need loving. This is often where we spend the most time on the healing mandala: finding what is really underneath our discovery, finding where the body sensation is really coming from.

Listening to your body and finding those sensations in your body will guide you quickly to how you are feeling, from simple hunger to the deepest longings of your soul. Your body holds all that information and will open up direct pathways if you are willing to let go of control and explore unconditionally, feeling the freedom of being right in the moment you are in.

Feelings are your guide to finding your path—they let you know if you are on your path—and you don't even have to identify the feeling or give it a story. In fact, labeling the feeling can sometimes separate you from presence and shut down your creativity. Instead of reinforcing an old, labeled version of yourself, you can just follow the energy of your feelings in your body, taking the time to be right in that moment and let the feelings move and breathe through you.

Notice where you are experiencing the feeling in your body. Notice what you are organizing your body around. Is it joy, pain, stress, ease? Try asking your body what it wants you to know. Often the feeling will shift and move, as you keep allowing the moments to unfold, and bring you back to center. Participating with what is happening, instead of managing or controlling it, will bring you home.

You don't always have to go to the old story of feeling sad or mad, which is often just a default position from the past. You can just let the energy of the feeling you are experiencing move in your body and notice the actual body sensations. As you notice the energy and allow it to move, it will take you to the next step or sometimes just dissipate.

As you move into this step of "Embracing," you are coming more into relationship with your own existence, something you may have lost in your journey through the stress and striving of negotiating your life. The exercises below are all gentle and fun ways to come back home to yourself.

"I Am Here"

I exist, I feel my being, my body, and I sing my song of "yes" to myself, creating song after song after song.

This simple and powerful practice is a quiet way to drop into your essence, very quickly, wherever you are, right in the moment. (www.turningthewheel.org/audio)

Take a walk outside in nature if you can before doing this for the first time. Give yourself a little time to listen to the soft sounds of the earth, the ones you don't always hear, like the rocks shifting, the breezes that are barely there, the sound of wings, the clouds slowly shifting. Maybe you can hear the waters of the earth flowing deep beneath your feet, or the footsteps of the little animals.

When you come back inside, bring that with you as you listen to the soft sounds of your own body and all the knowing you have just gathered.

Close your eyes and stand with both of your feet firmly on the earth, feeling the weight of each of your feet as you come to a quiet stillness in your body. Notice how your weight shifts back and forth, just a tiny bit, in order to keep you upright, and just relax into this soft rhythm, shifting gently from one foot to the other. Take a deep breath and sink a little further into your feet, feeling the earth coming up beneath you and around you to support you and hold you.

Place your hand on your heart and feel the shift in your body as this loving connection to yourself increases the flow of oxytocin in your body. Feel your breath coming in and out under your hand, through your heart, just gently breathing in through your heart and out through your heart. Each time you breathe in send some loving kindness to the beautiful being that is you in this moment, just as you are in this moment. As you breathe out, release any thoughts of ways you need to be fixed or changed, just letting them float away as you release the breath.

Bring your awareness back to your hand, feeling your feet on the ground again, and say out loud to yourself "I am here," letting your hand move down along the front of your body from your forehead down to the base of your spine as you speak. Do this three times slowly, maybe changing which word you emphasize each time.

As you are ready, blink open your eyes and take a step forward on the earth and say, "I am here." Keep walking slowly, and with each very intentional step, speak the words "I am here." Pause whenever you need to let the energy of those words flow into your body.

As you go, you may want do some looping with the earth, asking the earth, trees, sky, grasses, or water, to bless you. Then send your love and gratitude back to them for being here on the earth with us.

Try allowing the deep love of the mother earth to enter your body, coming up through your feet and traveling all around your body as you continue to say, either out loud or silently, "I am here."

You might want to add sounding from the center of the Earth. Just let the energy that is supporting you from the earth flow in through your feet, up your legs to your pelvis, into your belly and your lungs, through your heart and into your throat and finally out through your mouth. Go back and forth from feet to throat and play with the sounds as you walk and breathe well-being into your body. Go toward that which wants to be expressed.

Add the words "I am here" into your sounding as you find your own unique song that is filled with life and love.

As you are ready, come to stillness again and drop into the center of your body as you say to yourself, one last time, "I am here."

Walk around wherever you are and notice your energy and how your body feels. Take a few minutes to allow this shift to land.

The magic of this exploration is that you now have a reference experience in your body, and you can use this phrase any time you need to come home to your own story. Just quietly put your hand on your heart and say "I am here," and you will come back to your center and to your own song.

Facilitation Suggestions

It is important to give your participants time to integrate this experience through sharing how the experience was for them with a partner, and maybe making time for them to write in their journal.

After doing this a few times with a group, I add in phrases like the ones below for them to say as they do this meditative walk. Often the participants will have phrases of their own to add in, depending on what they are turning towards loving in themselves.

"I am here," "I see me," "I appreciate me."
"I am here," "I see me," "I am enough."
"I am here," "I see me," "I am loveable."

Radical Spontaneity

If you attend to what is happening in this moment and allow it to unfold—listening, playing, appreciating, releasing old stories, moving, and breathing—you can create an immediate new beginning. In fact, you can create spontaneous new discoveries hundreds of times a day and, subsequently, a life filled with new, fresh openings that are filled with aliveness. We call this radical spontaneity.

Remember, all attempts to control will only create suffering, whether you are attempting to control yourself or somebody else. We can so easily get stuck in a position and get very attached to that position, instead of truly knowing that we are all doing just exactly what we should be doing for our own evolution. I love the word "position" because it has an easy and immediate body solution. Just change the position of your body, move and breathe for a moment, and your attachment to your position will start dissolving, and your energy will start flowing. Suddenly you will see all kinds of possible, even radical, perspectives.

Raising seven kids has been an unrelenting and ongoing reminder of the power of appreciating what is happening in the moment and letting go of the illusion of control. Often what seemed like behavior that needed to be controlled was simply a cry for attention and help, and more often it was a reminder that I needed to attend to myself – to take a virtual break, get a snack or laugh and laugh!

Of course, the real miracle, and deepest learning, was that my children always knew what they really needed to be doing, whether it was studying, dancing, working, playing baseball, skiing, listening to loud music, being with friends, or doing nothing at all. I learned early on that they had their own body knowing and my best shot was to follow that and support it with a "yes, and..." response.

My favorite story illustrating this was when my granddaughter, Jayda, who was two years old at the time, was running around the room making a lot of noise and crashing into things. Cassandra (her mother) and I were trying to talk, and she was trying to be seen. Her very skilled and loving mother simply turned to her and said, "Honey, honey, if you want grandma to give you some attention, just ask her to and she will." My granddaughter stopped suddenly in the room and stood totally still, thinking about what her mom had said, and then she turned to me with fierce determination and said, while pointing her finger at her chest, "See me, Gramma!"

I still laugh every time I see her little face speaking such a deep and wonderful truth about what we all want. We often do something like this in our facilitator groups as we begin meetings or rehearsals: simply walking around the room all saying "See me," at the same time and pointing to our chests, just to get that truth on the table right from the start.

"Five Things"

Morgan, my youngest son and one of our enthusiastic and very energetic facilitators, taught us this game when we were in Wilmington, NC, and needed some magic to integrate the "posse of teens" who were performing with us. It is a great way to practice radical spontaneity, and it has become a standard for us ever since. Every group we play this with loves it. It is easy, really fun, and a quick way to warm up. You will need at least three friends to play this game with you. You can do it with your kids, your yoga class, or your

Spanish class. It will enliven any situation and infuse any group with energy and joy.

If you are working with a larger group, divide into small groups of four or five. To begin, you need to pick a theme that becomes a command that will be passed around the circle. The theme that you use for this can be anything from five things on your bedroom floor, to five things you see every morning, to five things you love about your mother, to five visions you have for your future. We use five things you love, or love about yourself a lot. You have to demonstrate this for it to make any sense. Just jump in and do it with your assistants once through and then it will be easy.

Once you have chosen the theme for the first round, then you choose somebody to start, and you say "John, tell me five things you love about yourself." John then calls out the first thing he can think of quickly and the group loudly says, "One" all together, as they raise their right hand up in the air to show support and joy. John then calls out the second thing he loves about himself and the group yells, "Two." When you reach "Five" the whole group calls out, "We have five things, HO," while gesturing with their arms in any direction they wish.

Then John passes it to the next person saying "Mary, tell me five things you love about yourself." And the whole thing begins again for Mary. Mary says what she loves about herself, and then the group all says "One," all the way through to "Five" and then "We have five things, HO!" Then Mary passes it on with the same sentence.

Throughout the whole game everyone is rapidly tapping their thighs over and over, like fast clapping, only on their thighs, and, if they wish, running in place with little steps as well. This keeps the energy and fast pace going and gives everyone enough exercise by the end to actually have some "feel good" neurotransmitters triggered.

Facilitation Suggestions

Your participants don't have to give an answer to the sentence that makes sense. They can just say anything that comes to mind. The idea is spontaneous response, not the content. So any word or phrase is great!

As we embrace this deeper level of spontaneous consciousness, we open up more channels of the mind-body connection and develop a more active relationship with our fluid cellular system. This inherently opens up our creative flow, which opens new pathways to finding our own gifts and happiness.

We used this in our work with a group of women in prison who were getting ready to be released in six months. At the end, we asked them what they had learned from it. Their answers were stunning—just a few minutes of play with so much gain!

"I learned that I can be silly and not worry about what others think about me."
"I learned that I love some things about myself."
"I laughed and had fun and I don't remember doing that for a long time."

"I felt how strong my body is. I kept running the whole time."

"I learned new things about people I have lived with for many years."

"I just feel really good right now"

"Rotating the Circle"

Another fun way to play spontaneously with a group is a game we call "Rotating the Circle." It goes in really well just after the group has finished changing places in the circle all at the same time by running across the circle to a new place. (See "Switching Places in the Circle," p. 298 in the "Resources" section.) We always start with "Switching Places" then have the whole group turn to the right and begin to move pretty quickly in a large circle, all rotating to the right together.

Now you can change places in this moving circle by running across the circle and getting behind somebody else. Anybody can go, so lots of people will be changing at the same time. Notice the space sharing and negotiation going on, especially in the center. You might just go behind the person who is behind you or you might run all the way across the circle to a new place.

Now change the direction the circle is rotating without pausing if you can, still changing places whenever you want.

As we build our community and connection to each other, let's make this game a little harder. Now five people must be changing at all times and no more than five—always five changing and never more than five. Just notice and respond in the moment.

Beautiful. This is really working. Now change the direction the circle is rotating again, and come back to just walking in the circle for a moment, feeling the solidarity of the group.

Whenever you want to change your place now you back across the circle, looking over your shoulder to be sure you are safe, and leading with your back. When you arrive back at the circle you go forward again with the group. Feel how different it is to lead with your back and let your body fill out a little into a more three-dimensional body. It can be good to back yourself up sometimes, to "have your own back."

Let's try one more piece of the game.

When anybody stops the rotation, everybody stops wherever they are, until somebody starts again. We are still changing places while doing this. And let's add in one more complication at the same time. When anybody changes the direction of the rotation of the circle, everybody changes.

Do both of these at the same time while still changing places whenever you want. Fabulous.

Notice if you think things need to change more, or if you think it is all changing too much, and see what happens if everybody is paying attention to that.

Now pause and give yourselves a big hand. That was amazing.

"Running Seeds"

Probably one of the easiest and most accessible spontaneous games we play is the "Seed" exercise. Effective and fun for every group and population, it offers deep learning in leadership, collaboration and group awareness. Here is one version that is fun, profound, and radical all at the same time. (The basic "Seed" exercise is fully explained on p. 275 in the "Resources" section of this book.)

Let your group know that the intention when we surround the seed person is to affirm and support them, responding to their shape, their energy, and their story very quickly and spontaneously. They are the seed that inspires our response. This is a fun combination of responding in your body in the moment and developing the facility to quickly see the other person and respond with your body in a way that paces them.

Start with everyone standing in a circle and do a demonstration. Ask one of your assistants to go in the middle of the circle and take a shape.

Linda is going to go in the middle of our circle and make a shape. She can take her time moving in the middle however she wants until she feels ready to land in a shape, and come to stillness. She could also just run in and land in any shape that happens. As soon as Linda, our "seed" person, is totally still, the rest of us are going to run in and take a shape in response to that seed shape and get very still. Ready, go.

Beautiful. Now we hold this shape until somebody new runs somewhere in the room, any place they want, and takes a new shape. There goes John. Now John is the seed, and the rest of us run after him and take a shape around him, all coming to stillness again—until the next person runs.

Once you have completed the demonstration, have your group create smaller circles of four or five people to play the game. It helps if you have someone in each group who has played the game before. After a while you can pause and let the groups watch each other, as it is really fun to watch and can be very poignant.

Once again, it helps to have fun and lively music for this. Very quickly, the participants begin to laugh and play. Without even knowing it, they are gaining new perceptions of themselves and others while moving and playing in the space.

Revealing Yourself to Yourself

One fun key to the "Embracing" step on the mandala is to reconnect with your awe-filled curiosity, your childlike joy at discovering something new, unexpected, and surprising. Our brain loves something fresh and spontaneous. And keeping curiosity alive helps us stay flexible and adaptable so we can keep letting go of old perceptions and ideas and welcome new ones into our story.

The power of making connections in the brain is awe-inspiring. Our amazing brain is constantly making connections based on our experiences and then creating patterns based on those experiences: nurture not nature. You are literally in charge of who you are by what you are telling your brain, wiring your own story moment by moment. Before you were even born you were creating these connections, literally forming your mind—networking your self—link by link. And your brain is listening all the time, ready and willing to be rewired right now, thought by thought.

Asking yourself questions with genuine curiosity and wonder is one easy and fun way to do this. I love this idea of a wonder question because it integrates a sort of gentle kindness. You get to hang out in your innocence for a bit and surprise yourself. This is about revealing yourself to yourself. Just let it all flow—skip the editing, which will take you away from your authenticity—and enjoy the wonder of your own consciousness and wisdom.

Genuine wonder begins by getting grounded in your body and letting your "body knowing" guide you to an answer. Remember to keep moving and breathing as you go. You might ask yourself questions like "I wonder how I am feeling right now?" or "I wonder what I want right now? Then answer the question in all kinds of fun ways that allow you to create new patterns and new possibilities.

So, for example, you might answer in movement or sound, or with a song or a drawing, or maybe in gibberish, a made-up language improvised right in the moment! You might answer as if you were the sounds of the strings on a violin or the beats of a drum, or as if you were running a very fast race and out of breath. You might actually run while you answer, or go for a fast walk or a stroll. The trick is to have fun, and then the guardian of the portal will let you through and you will have your answer to your question.

I learned this technique of asking yourself questions a long time ago in a psychodrama exercise, but it wasn't meant to be so fun and gentle. Katie Hendricks, an international seminar leader (www.hendricks.com) and an ongoing transformative guide in my life, named these questions "wonder questions"—a great frame for this process—and I love the name. It is a cue to be gentle with yourself: just wondering, not beating yourself up for not knowing the answer or for not having looked at this before or for having looked at it way too many times. Just take a moment and a nice deep breath and wonder. Then start moving, playing, or making sound however you want. Astonishingly, you always get an answer, and it is always interesting.

Wonder Questions to Get You Started

I wonder what my body is telling me?

I wonder what needs loving in me?

I wonder what I want right now?

I wonder what my heart is telling me right now?

I wonder what I am feeling right now?

I wonder what I am organizing my thoughts around right now?

I wonder what I want to turn towards?

I wonder what is motivating me right now?

I wonder what part of me is in charge right now?

I wonder if this is something I have done before?

I wonder if this is something I have felt before?

I wonder what would feel good to me right now?

I wonder what I am making up right now?

I wonder who I am loving right now?

I wonder who is loving me right now?

Add your own!

"Finding and Moving Your Signature Sound"

This exercise, another beautiful way to reveal yourself to yourself, was taught to me more than 20 years ago by an amazing and gifted sound healer named Vickie Dodd (www.sacredsoundschool.com). It is a powerful portal to your inner landscape and an amazing tool for a quick connection back to center. Though I have changed it some over the years, the basic essence has stayed the same, which is to tune into yourself and embrace your own energy field so you can show up authentically in the moment, feeling safe and clear. From there you can literally extend your reach out all the way around the world and back again, if you wish. (You can listen to the audio recording at www.turningthewheel.org/audio.)

Before beginning this journey with your group, bring everyone together in a circle to check in for a minute. Ask them to turn to a partner next to them and share something they appreciate about themselves right in this moment. After each person has had a turn, bring the group back to the circle and begin.

We are going to do an exercise to find and move inside our signature sound—that is the sound that is uniquely ours in this moment. We will find this sound by speaking our name over and over until our name drops into our mouths and becomes a tone that is simply the tone we were speaking. This sounds harder than it is, so just go ahead and start saying your name and let it move inside your mouth and move it around in there, letting it turn itself into a tone. I will do it first to show you what it looks like.

As you begin to find your tone for this moment, let it become a hum and circulate it through your whole body, into your fingertips and up to the top of your head and down to the bottom of your feet. Feel it vibrating in your whole body.

Keep humming and now begin to walk around the room as you hum, feeling your feet firmly on the ground supported by the energy from the center of the earth. Keep your hum circulating as you walk through the room—completely focused on your own body and hum and field of energy, using your hum to create a kinesthetic field around you.

Slowly, as you are ready, begin to extend your hum out around your body in a circle that is as big as the span of your arms—as far as your arms can reach—what I call your "kinesphere." Let your hum surround and bathe your body, keeping this expanded energy field all to yourself for now.

When you are ready play with sending your field out further and then bringing it back close to you again. Expand your field as big and wide as you want and then bring it back in close again. See if you can expand your energy across the plains or the mountains—maybe even all the way around the world and back again. We actually have the ability to do that without much effort if we wish. Just see it happening and it will, traveling on the molecular reality that we are all one beautiful pool of moving energy.

Humming to Health

This exercise changed my life and started me on my path towards connecting to and embracing my body in a loving and healthy way. At the time I was the mother of seven children, preparing a family dinner every night, running my graphic design firm, going to school part time for my master's degree, teaching my movement classes, taking several dance classes a week, supporting the man who was my husband then, both emotionally and financially, and preparing to tour a huge community performance piece to the Seattle Fringe Festival.

I had very little sense of who I was, separate from all those projects and people and their needs. Though I was generally happy most of every day—I loved being a mother and had lots of energy for my work—I was definitely wearing myself out, losing weight, struggling with allergies and viruses, and working late into the night in order to have my daytime hours with my kids.

Many people had told me that I needed to slow down, do less, take care of myself, and so forth, which only made me work harder to prove to them that I could do it all. For me, one of the benefits, and at the same time the downside, of being an abused child was to become an overachiever. I obviously needed some healing, but—like everybody else on the planet—I did not want to be fixed!

Working with sound was miraculous. There was no language to get bogged down in, and Vickie did not tell me what I should or should not be doing. She simply began healing the layers of my body with her shamanistic sound and helping me energetically disconnect from some old stories and relationships from my past so I could begin to make space for myself.

I started using my signature sound before going to sleep every night and first thing every morning. I hummed silently in meetings if I was getting scared or triggered, and I hummed out loud with the kids while making dinner. I hummed while I worked and while I played. I hummed a whole new layer of me into existence and a whole new part of my authentic soul's journey emerged.

And as I released more of the old stories and loved myself a little more, I did make changes in my life to create a healthier, more-balanced rhythm of work and rest.

Body to Body, Moment to Moment

My heart beats with the fullness of the sky, holding all of us under one very alive and infinite canopy.

All of life is about relating to ourselves and to each other. Virtually all of our suffering is related to what we have learned about that and what we then tell ourselves is true.

Once we can witness all of ourselves with loving attention in a sustained way, adding in noticing how we relate to others will come naturally. It starts happening automatically, as you see others through fresh, clear, loving eyes. You can get curious about what takes you into connection and what takes you out, and even more importantly, you can gather the data for where these different responses live in your body.

There are many forms we do in pairs in our work and they are such a rich and fertile ground for exploring how we interact with others when all language is dropped out. I call this "Body to Body, Moment to Moment." In the simple exercises below, many of which are adapted from my years in contact improvisation and modern dance, you will find all you need to build a healthy relationship with practically anyone.

Contained in any duet are all the basic relationship negotiations of cooperation and influence, attraction and impulse, balance and contrast, initiation and response, and close and far. But that is not all. A really meaningful duet will have kindness, generosity, tenderness, and even moments of stillness and quiet. The whole process of moving together, responding to each other, and really seeing each other is a profound dialog that once learned in the body can manifest in many different ways and places in your life.

More duet explorations, including "Leading Blind and Sculpting" and "Touching Lightly," can be found in the "Resources" section (p. 267 and p. 301 respectively).

"This Is Me, This Is You"

I celebrate the starlight shining in my soul, as I see the light of the heavens circling your heart.

This exercise is a simple little piece of magic that creates so much loving connection in a group that you can feel the hearts beating in the air around you. Here is how it goes.

Find a partner and find your space in the room where you will stand and face each other to begin. Take a moment to just be there together noticing yourself and your breath. In this exercise you will both speak the same words at the same time as you move your hands in a gesture that reflects what you are saying.

The words you are saying together are "This is you" as you gesture at the other person's heart and "This is me" as your hand returns to your own heart.

Let's begin. Looking into each other eyes, place your hand on your heart and say, "This is me" at the same time as your partner, and then reach your hand out towards your partner in a gesture toward his or her heart saying, "This is you," at the same time as your partner.

Just keep doing this, letting it deepen into your body a little more each time.

"This is me." "This is you."
"This is me." "This is you."

As you keep repeating it, the energy may change from serious and intimate to more rowdy and moving—like jumping up and down and saying "This is me, this is me, this is me," before going back over to the other person. You may also stay very quiet the whole time. Let it become a dance between you and your partner.

Facilitation Suggestions

This very tender and intimate connection can be inserted at the end of many different explorations to gently land your participants back in their own bodies and in sweet connection to each other.

"Gesture Mirroring"

Often we don't really look at each other very much or see all different parts of another person. We have been trained that it is rude to stare or to really look at each other. This is unfortunate because everything we need to know about somebody can be found in his or her body language. We tend to fall in love with people that we really see, no matter what the story or relationship.

For many couples or friends this is a great exploration in noticing your roles and preferences in initiating and responding, often an area of conflict for partnerships of all kinds.

In this very fun game you are simply copying a gesture your partner does as closely as you can, remembering that you also always take care of yourself and your body.

Find a partner and decide who is going to make the first gesture. In this game you will take turns being the leader and the follower. If you are the first leader, begin by just letting any gesture come up from your body. Follower, you just copy it to the best of your ability. Now if you were the follower, you make a gesture and your partner feeds it back to you. Keep switching back and forth, feeding your partner's gestures back to them as accurately as you can.

The gestures can be slow and intense or quick and silly. They can move you through the room or be in one place. They can be big or little, choppy or smooth. Just have fun. Take turns seeing each other.

As you go along it may become harder and harder to tell who is copying who. One of you may end up leading for a minute or two and then handing it back to the other. Have fun. Just let this little back and forth dance go wherever it goes.

I believe that this very simple and playful exercise has the possibility to change the lives of those who get to participate almost immediately. We have seen dramatic change in our youth who play a whole menu of these kinds of games with us as they rediscover their intelligence and their leadership ability. Just having someone copy what you are doing is powerful in and of itself.

Because I didn't have a safe container growing up, this issue of initiating versus responding was central for me. The safest thing to do was to become invisible, so I was always defaulting to response, to hiding. And my attempts to initiate were often aggressive and filled with fear and fight. I still remember vividly the times I initiated and was punished swiftly and violently.

Sorting the Eggs

One of my jobs was to sort the eggs that we gathered from about 500 chickens and then sold to neighbors. First they had to be weighed to determine if they were small, medium, large, or extra large, and then they had to be put into the appropriate carton. It was a boring job, and I was always making up ways to make it go faster or to make it more efficient. I was using my intelligence to make the job more interesting and initiating new ways to do the job. In TTW we call this a "thread of health" coming through.

When my father saw what I was doing, his rage was immediate and his violence swift. I wasn't doing the task the way he had told me to do it. I knew he was wrong and, at the same time, I also learned the lesson in my body that innovation and initiation were dangerous, and that they were not going to be tolerated.

In contrast to this experience, when my son Lucas was two-and-a- half years old, we were walking through an apartment complex to a friend's house and we passed by a swimming pool. Lucas saw the pool and immediately took a long running leap right into the water.

It took me a minute to figure out what had happened, and then I leaped in after him in my clothes, shoes and all and pulled him out holding him tightly to my chest. He could not swim and I was really frightened for a moment and then very wet and very grateful that he was OK.

Though many well meaning folks said I should punish him, and be sure he understood the danger of what he had done and how much he had frightened me, I knew that he had not meant to do anything wrong. I also knew that I could have been holding his hand as we were walking and it wouldn't have happened at all.

And most important I knew that that jump in the pool was like my sorting the eggs my way -- it was his initiator, his "go for it" spirit, which needed to be maintained, possibly made a little wiser, but not punished. Thirty-seven years later, he is an innovative, creative thinker, still occasionally jumping in pools, and finding his own way to success. I am glad I did not try to subdue or control that impulsive, courageous, energetic force in his story.

Our ability to initiate is tightly linked to innovation and to our empowered creative energy. I learned to allow this back into my life by allowing it to manifest in my children and by dancing and dancing and dancing until my inner joy could merge with my very creative and active brain.

I have since witnessed this need to be right and in control that I experienced with my father in thousands of subtle and not so subtle ways in myself, and in countless classrooms and boardrooms and families and relationships across the country. It is directly linked to how much we have (or have not) come into a positive relationship to ourselves, and to how much we have (or have not) manifested our own story.

"Sequential Mirroring"

This exercise is an opportunity to initiate and speak with your body and respond to your partner directly from your body wisdom. It is also a chance to really be seen and to practice witnessing another person without judgment. I have worked with many couples that have healed old stories they had created with friends or partners simply by dropping out the language and communicating through movement only.

Find a partner and decide who will be the mover first and who will be the witness. The mover is going to move for 60 seconds, and the witness is going to move whatever he or she remembers from witnessing her partner.

Witness, try listening with your whole body—all of your senses including your skin and from all different parts of your body. Listen with your gut, your hands, your heart, your back, and your breath. The idea is not to memorize what your mover is doing, but just to see what sticks with your body and, even more important, how your body wants to respond to what you have just witnessed.

Mover, you can just let your body say whatever it wants to, without thinking about it or trying to form it in any way. You might even surprise yourself. Just drop down into your feet and your breath and see what is there today. Don't worry about your watcher being able to remember it.

This is about speaking together from one body to another, hopefully bypassing the interpretive function for a moment and letting your body respond to this beautiful being in front of you with total authenticity.

Let's begin. Everyone get a partner and spread out into the room.

Mover, go ahead and start moving in any way you want, just enjoying following your body and relaxing into the moment. I will let you know to pause after about one minute.

Time one minute and then gently call say:

Pause.

Witness, reflect back to your partner—in movement—anything you saw or felt while witnessing your partner. Mover, you get to enjoy this reflection and bask in the good attention you are receiving.

Without talking about what just happened, switch who is the mover and the witness, and I will time one minute of movement for the new mover.

Time one minute and then gently call say:

Pause.

Witness, now it is your turn to just reflect back to your partner— in movement—anything you saw or felt while witnessing your partner. Mover, now you get to enjoy this reflection and bask in the good attention you are receiving.

Take a few minutes to talk to your partner and share how that was for you, especially anything you may have discovered in the process.

Alana Shaw

Facilitation Suggestions

I do a quick demonstration before beginning this to be sure that the group understands the sequence and the intent. It is easy to get caught in trying to memorize and duplicate exactly what you have seen, when the point is more about responding from your body to their body, rather than duplicating.

"Seeing with Eyes Closed"

This exercise asks us to go even deeper into our intuitive selves and to tune into our partner with a degree of sensitivity that many of us have never done with anybody, not even our lovers or children. It automatically creates connection and trust on both the mover's and the watcher's parts. It is a sweet little dip into other ways of knowing.

Often when we are afraid or worried, we go inside ourselves and only pay attention to our own feelings and confusion. We get caught up in our inner drama and don't take in enough information from the people around us. If we remember to look outside of ourselves and use all of our senses and powers of gathering information, our whole perception of a situation will change. The more we develop our ability to see and understand others, the less time we will spend making up stories about what is going on with them or with us.

In this exercise we get to explore speaking to each other from our body energies without using our eyes. You will have a chance to play with listening with other sensors in your body, activating and making conscious new ways of gathering information.

Find a partner. One of you is going to move and the other is going to watch with your eyes closed. Decide who will move first.

Mover, you move however you want, staying close to your partner, for about 30 seconds. I will tell you when to start and when to pause and bring your movement to a close. You are talking with your body to your partner and sending them loving connection.

Let's begin.

Watcher, stand quietly with your eyes closed, breathing and relaxing into your body in this moment. Let your energy expand and open to include your partner. Listen to them with your whole body. Notice what you feel in your body as you listen with your heart, your skin, your belly, your breath…

Mover, begin moving.

Time 30 seconds and then gently say:

Pause.
(You may choose to allow additional time, depending on your group and their experience.)

Movers, bring your movement gently to a close.

Watcher, you now reflect back in movement what you "saw," just gently dropping in and letting your body express to your mover, sharing what you sensed or felt as you listened with love to your partner.

Without talking yet, switch roles, and those of you who just moved, close your eyes and your partner will move for you this time.

Mover, begin moving.

Time 30 seconds and then gently say:

Pause.

Movers, bring your movement gently to a close.

Watcher, you now reflect back in movement what you "saw," just gently dropping in and letting your body express to your mover, sharing what you sensed or felt as you listened with love to your partner.

That was beautiful. The focus and connection was so inspiring to witness. Take a few minutes and talk with your partner about how that was for you.

Touch Exercises

Touch is one of our very basic human needs, and there are many fears associated with touch in today's culture. We have essentially made it wrong to touch each other outside of our primary relationships. These exercises are a safe and comfortable way to explore touch and gentle contact.

"Alternating Hands"

Just start walking in the room, breathing and releasing, sighing, making sound if you wish and shaking out any tension or stories you are holding on to in the moment. Notice your body sensations and give a little loving attention to any place that is tight or painful and let it release.

As you are walking and moving start noticing others in the room. You might try something you see someone else doing or have a quick little moving interaction with someone as you pass by. Keep going and add in "touch and go." Just gently and appropriately touch someone as you pass by and then the next person and the next, weaving some gentle connections into the room. There is no right or wrong way to do this. It is just to have fun, to get present in the room, and to get your body warmed up.

As you are moving through the room, let yourself land with a partner and say hello to them in movement however you wish.

Now one of you reach out and gently touch the other person, letting your hand stay there until you feel you have made a connection with the energy of the place you are touching. Then just remove you hand. As your partner removes their hand, you reach out to gently return the touch. Let this begin slowly, taking your time without getting stuck, letting the alternating of touch just flow easily from one to the other.

Keep going and let this turn into a fun dance of playful connection. You might respond with touch before a person has stopped touching you. You might speed it up and move through the room together. It might turn into tapping for some of you, bouncing through the room, or into a sustained slow touch with others that winds your bodies together. Again, there is no right way to do this. Your body knows what it wants to do and what is fun and comfortable for you and your partner.

Take a few minutes to find your ending to this dance, taking your time to complete. Check in with your partner and see how that was for him or her.

Facilitation Suggestions

I start this with quiet music, and then let it turn in to something more fun and playful. It helps folks feel safe and maybe not take it too seriously or get too self-conscious.

"Making Contact—Seeing and Responding"

I first did this exercise or game while working with Contraband, a San Francisco Dance Company, one summer in a particularly rich workshop at the Colorado Dance Festival. It was a powerful change point for me as being seen and certainly being randomly touched held a lot of potential to retrigger my childhood body memories. Instead it was very healing and freeing to experience touch in play and fun with literally no agenda.

This is an amazing exercise for practicing witnessing in the moment, while giving the body a safe experience in trust—trusting itself and trusting others.

Find a partner and introduce yourself if you don't know each other. If you came with your significant other, this is a great one to do together. Choose who will be the mover and who will follow to start. We will switch, so both of you will get a chance to do both parts.

Mover, you just head out shaping and moving your way into the room, moving however you want, just relaxing and letting your body lead. You are going to be taking cues from your follower, who will stay close to you as you move through the room.

Follower, your job is to move along beside the mover, at first just noticing how they move, where they seem to mostly initiate their movement from, where they seem to not be moving much, where they have spontaneous impulses in their body. Do they move mostly forward, or sideways or backwards sometimes? Do they turn or twist or swing or rest? You are just taking a little time to appreciate the uniqueness and beauty of their story in motion, and to give them some good attention.

Follower, when you feel ready you will begin just gently touching with a moment of firm pressure some place on the mover's body to bring attention there. Do this intuitively as you move along beside them, not worrying about why, but trusting your body to speak to their body in the perfect way for both of you. You just keep doing this for as long as they are moving—noticing how often you want to touch by watching the responses of your mover. They may need time to respond and they may be very quick. You will want to give them time to land their response to your touch and then to return to their own story for a moment before they respond to you again.

Mover, you now get to have the fun of responding to that touch by moving towards the touch with the part of the body that was touched. And from the impulse of that response see where the movement goes and how it completes. Each touch is an invitation to shift into that part of your body, to shift towards that direction, and to follow that shift until it lands and you return to your own impulses.

Remember this is a duet—a loving co-creation. For the follower, part of the fun is seeing how finely you can tune yourself to the rhythms of your partner and how beautifully your timing can mesh with their timing and flow.

For the mover, your movement is being partially guided by someone else, so this is a really fun opportunity to let yourself surrender to that, letting it be the impetus for fun and for learning and for new movement possibilities. This is an amazing exercise in teaching the body about trust. It gives you a reference point in motion for trusting your self and opening to new possibilities with others.

Step III
Loving "The Body Now"
Loving, Empowering, Reclaiming

Affirmation: I am ready to align my body with what I know in my heart and to embrace my fully embodied "yes" to loving myself and manifesting my sacred gifts.

I am struck every day by how much the real passion of our lives is found in remembering that we are loved and that we are here to love. As I breathe into my heart through each day, I am further reminded that those memories live absolutely and profoundly in the very fluids and muscles and bones of our bodies.

This next step on our healing cycle is the one that fully lands this knowing in our bodies and creates the harmony that prevails when the past and the present and the future show up as one. Only the body knows how to do this—and does it gracefully and without effort.

If we are measuring our progress by how deeply we embrace our own goodness and believe in the innate goodness of all beings, then what we can create, and the impact we can have with our time here on the earth will be immeasurable, and we will be unstoppable.

This wonderful step of falling in love with all of who you are moves you directly into authenticity, opening up all the portals of the universe for everything you ever dreamed of. And the commitment to unconditionally loving yourself instantly expands your capacity to give love and to receive love, a crucial step in reclaiming all of who you are. The circle, which begins with looping love out, cannot complete itself if you don't loop back in and receive the love that is there for you.

You know you are home to your own well-being, that you are remembering well, by the way your body feels, that easy feeling of well-being streaming through your organs, your limbs, and your blood. Your breath feels centered and balanced, instead of fast and high. You may even feel a deeper sense of connection to other people and an easy connection to your version of a loving source, or your higher self.

The Gift of Loving Self

Your willingness to be awake to your body and to love all of who you are is an incredible gift you are giving yourself and those around you. It is crucial to let yourself move on into this step on the mandala and ride the joy of surrendering to the truth of your magic and to the truth of your beautiful sacred gifts that you are here to manifest. The survival of our astounding planet earth and all the humans and animals, and nature and spirits that surround us depends on it.

Once you move into this third step of loving on the healing cycle, the last step of acting and releasing just flows right in. So often after an awakening experience, we move to the second step and really do embrace its truth and impact, and then start trying to change and fix ourselves almost immediately. This may seem like we are taking action, but it will unconsciously trigger resistance, which stops our progress and puts us into drama and failure. So we end up just moving back and forth between the first two steps on the mandala, seeking more insights that will help us change.

Instead, when we have awakened to and embraced a new understanding or perception about ourselves or our past, we can step into well-being and into the positive change we want, by moving on around the mandala and asking ourselves: "What needs loving here?" The actions that come out of this strategy will be filled with releasing and allowing, and the action steps we create will take us into honoring ourselves more and creating a space for taking care of ourselves. (See "Spiraling into the Body Now" on p. 292 in the "Resources" section.)

Almost always it will be an inner child who needs to be loved and seen (and acknowledged and empowered) before he or she will let you move on. It could be some gift you left behind as a child that wants to be reclaimed, a piece of your story you don't want to turn towards, or a part of yourself you have been particularly critical of for a long time. When I first discovered this step, I moved through what seemed like lifetimes of issues at record speed.

Because of so many memories that were triggered by my father's death, I had been hanging out on the healing Mandala for two long days, moving and breathing through my sadness and fear, reaching for some key that would open up the next level of freedom for me. I had reconnected with how afraid I am of anger—my own and others'—and spent time with my "inner eight-year-old girl," who was scared all the time and who could still jump into the forefront and take charge of me.

As my sweet friend Holly reminded me, that little girl is very tender, and she also knows a lot about positive, optimistic, enthusiastic loving, so I want to keep her in my story, letting her share her innocence with me. I want to let my "body now"—my breathing, my moving, and my knowing —show up to ally with her. I want to let her know that I will take care of her and protect her now, so she can come into a secure and happy place inside me.

Alana Shaw

I had moved through the healing cycle several times, going from just feeling the sensation of the fear in my gut and moving with that sensation (Awakening), to uncovering the source of the fear (Embracing), to loving myself and my little girl—rocking her and letting her know that I am here now and protecting her, and recognizing and loving the gifts of compassion and clarity all of my experiences have given me (Loving), to finally letting go, through an action step of moving and laying on the earth or singing and sounding and moving until I felt a shift and release in my body (Acting).

During one of these trips around the mandala, I remembered a very poignant experience in my life that turned out to be an important key to unlocking my residual resistance to taking care of myself. It came through in brilliant, living Technicolor as if I were there again.

The Ice Cream Cone

I was eight years old and had gone with my mother on a shopping trip, and while she was getting groceries I walked around the shopping center with a nickel in my pocket that I had brought along to buy something. I had earned the nickel selling rhubarb (that I cut and washed and packaged with rubber bands) to the neighbors and very much thought it was mine to spend. My little sister and I were allowed to keep that rhubarb money in our banks.

I ended up at the creamery and found out that a single dip ice cream cone was a nickel. I had never bought an ice cream

128

at the store and was very excited to order my cone and pay by myself and walked out licking my ice cream in a state of near euphoria. I had almost finished my cone when my mother came out to the car and exploded in anger when she saw what I had done.

She was furious about my independent act and told me I would be switched with a limb from the mulberry tree when I got home. I was terrified and confused by her response. All the way home she lectured me about being selfish and thinking only of myself and that it was bad and wrong to buy an ice cream for myself when my brothers and sisters (there were six of us) were not going to have one too. She said she couldn't imagine what I was thinking and that I should have known better, a particularly biting shame. Unless I could buy enough to share with everybody, I was not to buy any at all. I did get switched until the backs of my legs were red with welts while the other kids watched my shame, a lesson for them as well as me.

I had been carrying this story in my body from that day on, and in many ways it was a guiding principle of my life. I think the physical punishment with witnesses served to anchor the story and the lesson in my body very deeply. I had remembered this experience when I was in my twenties and looked at ways it was impacting my life, but I didn't have any way to go any further with it. Putting it on the healing cycle was so exciting and powerful for me, actually moving it through to a new place where it could lose its charge. As part of my action step, I gathered my friends around me for support, which was a sign of healing already as I was asking for what I wanted, asking for help.

We spent a beautiful afternoon loving my little girl; moving, hugging, sounding, crying, and laughing as we unraveled the story in my body and looked at how my mother's own unhappiness and deprivation was played out through me.

It was a great reminder for me that awakening to what is going on and being willing to embrace it is not enough. We must keep going thorough the mandala to the third step of loving ourselves and everything just the way it is right now, accepting the experience enough to take action and move all the way to releasing the contraction and fluid restriction that my body was carrying forward around this experience.

As I moved through to the end of the cycle, I felt the reward of a whole new level of freedom and openness in my body, allowing me to come with more alignment into being present and then more present, following my body into living a life where I remembered that I can have what I want and truly embrace a flow of "What wants to happen now?"

Facilitation Suggestions

One important piece to remember as you are moving and playing on the mandala is that it is not helpful to hang out anywhere on the healing cycle for too long and so re-traumatize yourself. Living an experience over and over again does not heal the wound. Just keep moving on the cycle, and moving and breathing as you go, loving what needs loving, and feel the ease with which you can evolve and feel good.

If you start to feel stuck or see that people in your group are getting stuck, you can shift out of that energy by getting folks moving again. Take a break for a walk outside, or do the "Rocking in the Arms of Love" exercise (p. 166). You could simply suggest that everyone stand up and walk around (or do this yourself if you are working alone). You could also find a partner and share something you appreciate about yourself with this partner.

Revealing Self to Other

One of the wonderful rewards of loving more and more parts of yourself is that you have less and less to hide and to defend and justify. I was conditioned in my body to defend in order to survive, and I spent much of my young life stuck in that mode. Though I can still have that response, I no longer always have to act on it. Being able to show up just as you are and to trust that you will be enough and be lovable too, is one key to a stress-free flow through your days.

A really important threshold experience for me was realizing that an unedited me would do much less damage than an edited me. It was like my whole brain rewired itself in 10 seconds. As we have already seen, I learned very young that speaking out was dangerous. I came to believe that editing myself and being careful what I say and what I reveal was the answer to keeping myself safe. I also believed that it was an essential part of being a grown-up, that acting appropriately was the clear path to maturity and respect.

One day, out of the blue, the message finally broke through. As long as I am revealing information, requests, or feelings that I am experiencing, the people around me are safe. It is when I start not saying, and not telling, that I become toxic and dangerous. I will leak little criticisms and make indirect blames, and have "stillness" around my love and acceptance and certainly my generosity of spirit. I will be caught in my own snare of unfelt and unexpressed feelings, and others will get caught in there with me.

We had an experience in our TTW group where one of our team was withholding feelings of unhappiness and anger and then blaming others. As this story got shared in private conversations, it became empowered as truth and suddenly everybody was talking about everybody else behind their backs, a clear agreement we had rarely broken before then. I was amazed at the depth of stillness and dysfunction that rose rapidly up to meet us—how quickly those old neurological patterns would show up even in a group that was committed to taking responsibility for our own story. Once the projection was on the table it was easy to move to a new place, to love each other, and to create some useful action steps.

Hiding inside ourselves is so exhausting and debilitating, and so easily shifted by simply jumping on the healing cycle and waking up, either to what you are afraid of or to what you want right now that you have not turned towards. Then you get to love that piece and take an action step out of suffering. It can take as little as a minute to withdraw your projections from others and restore yourself to ease and integrity.

"Revealing a Layer"

This is a simple way to play with letting go of hiding from yourself and others and "revealing" in your body through movement, without the complication of words. It is beautiful to watch and lovely and freeing to do.

Once again, you can do this on your own or in a group. The script below is written for a group but can be used for either one. An audio guide for individual exploration can be found online (www.turningthewheel.org/audio).

Begin by walking in the room and feeling your own body in the space. Notice the space between you and others in the room and let that flow and change comfortably.

Scan your body for places that feel contracted and just visualize some space opening up around those places and let them expand into the space you have created.

Feel your body grow wider and taller as you open up space in your body for your fluids to flow easily through and bath you in their healing balm.

As you are walking, begin to see layers of old stories and stress in your body that are floating to the surface, ready for you to see them and love them and release them back to where they came from.

Alana Shaw

Thank them as you release them for all they taught you and loop some love and appreciation to them as they float away. You don't even have to know what you are revealing or releasing, just trust that your body will know.

Reach over as you are walking and peel a layer off of your arm or the top of your head. Maybe you will pull a layer out of your eye or your ear - something you saw or heard that you are ready to release.

Let yourself hum and sound as you are walking if you wish, and try reaching down and brushing a layer off your legs that you have been holding in those muscles.

Maybe you want to rub or caress your belly to release a story you have been carrying in your gut, one that keeps triggering the same "gut response" over and over again.

Remember, you don't have to know the content of what you are releasing, just trust that your body will know.

In between revealing and releasing, you can just walk slowly through the room and rest into that freedom you have just created by revealing that judgment or sensation to yourself and to others, and releasing it.

Tune in to your breath and your fluids, and notice how you are feeling as you keep brushing and pulling and caressing and loving yourself out of these old stories. As the fluids of your cells are restored to movement, you can actually feel a sense of energy being released and freed in your body.

When you are ready, find a partner to play with and remember the joy of support and love in community. Without actually touching, sweep each other off a little and brush away some of the cobwebs from your partner and allow your partner to lovingly and playfully sweep your energy field too.

Let this playfulness turn into a "moment to moment" duet as the authentic movement of this newfound freedom emerges into the room. Fill the room with sound and freedom and play as you embody the lightness of soul you have just created by your own willingness.

Facilitation Suggestions

When you feel the group has completed the exercise, bring them back together in a circle and do a "Copy Circle," a "Sounding Circle," or sing a joyful chant together to close. (See pp. 262, and 281 in the "Resources" section.)

We are born with our gifts in place, ready to emerge and unfold as we grow and are nurtured in love. Along the way, for many of us, these treasures get buried beneath cultural stories and myths that we are conditioned by and rewarded for conforming with.

We are conditioned to function from denying ourselves the things we want instead of going after what we do want and making it so. We tell ourselves what we cannot eat, should not do, cannot afford, do not have time for, or cannot risk. These very things become our deepest longings, and we are set up to be unhappy. We turn towards others for our happiness, hoping they will fill in the longing. They can't, of course, and so we eventually blame them for our unhappiness.

All of this can be bypassed by allowing those pieces of our puzzle to be revealed and then by living our lives by asking ourselves affirming and loving questions: "What wants to happen in this moment?" "What is my body telling me right now?" What do I want right now?"

Listening to Voice of the Earth—Soul Retrieval

The mystical journey that follows is another way to listen to our bodies and step out of old conditioning that no longer serves us. It is another way to gather information that will support us in moving forward in our lives to more ease and joy.

As we navigate through the complexities of our lives, we leave parts of our soul behind. We have very good reasons for doing this at the time: our very survival, in some cases, or the need for love, approval, and acceptance, in most cases. Reclaiming our lost pieces restores our empowered wholeness and is ultimately of service to the evolution of our species.

Twenty years ago I had the privilege of taking a workshop with a Native American storyteller from the Northwest Coast named Johnny Moses. In his tradition, when you leave those pieces behind, the earth holds them for you until you are ready to retrieve them.

The inspiration for the meditation journey below was one of the many gifts of wisdom he gave us that week. It is another way to listen to our bodies and to the earth at the same time, or maybe to our spirit guides.

"Receiving the Gift"

You may want to write in your journal at the end of this meditation, so it would be helpful if you put your pen and paper out where you can easily get to them.

Begin by walking in the room and tuning into your own body sensations, giving some good attention to your fluids and your breath. You might want to say "I am here" (see p. 92) a few times and move and sound a little to get fully present in this moment.

As you are walking, drop even more into your own space, and let your body take you to a beautiful place in nature that nurtures you and makes you happy, maybe a meadow filled with flowers, a trail along a stream in the mountains, an open prairie with grasses blowing gently in the wind, a sandy beach along the ocean on a warm day...

This could be a place you have been or sometimes go, or an imaginary place you would like to go. Keep walking until you experience yourself in that space. Notice how the air feels, and the color of the sky.

Feel your feet on the earth, and as you are walking listen to the sounds of the earth and the beings around you: the birds, the stones, the water, the trees, and the grasses. Feel how supported and loved you are by this place.

As you are walking and listening, the earth will quietly ask you to pause, your body will know when to do this, maybe by a tide pool or under an ancient tree, in a pocket of yellow flowers, or just right along the path. Bend down in that place, and open your heart to receive a gift from the earth, something you left behind that you are ready to reclaim.

Take your time receiving this gift and thanking the earth spirits, maybe closing your eyes and staying there for a bit. Then slowly begin walking out of this land and back into the room, taking all the time you need to travel back into the present time in your body.

After you have had a chance to settle, you may want to find your journal and write or draw whatever is coming up for you.

Facilitation Suggestions

If you are leading a group you can close by slowly and quietly gathering your group into one circle of support by just reaching your hands out, inviting them to return to the to the circle of love and support that is there in the room for them. Then you can stand together in silence for a few moments if you like.

Start a "Sounding Circle" (p. 281 in the "Resources" section), cueing your group to create a song of their connection to each other and their loving connection to the earth.

Now gently guide your group to make their way to their journals, without talking, and write or draw about their experience, and anything that is coming up for them from this journey.

Finally, when everyone has had a chance to journal, let them know, in one outbreath, how incredible it was for you to get to witness such integrity and authenticity, and suggest that they make their way to a partner to share with each other and to give and receive some support.

Uncovering Your Treasure Chest

Curiously, no matter what we think we are looking at or responding to, we are actually only looking at and responding to ourselves.

Breaking the learned habit of hiding our true selves is crucial if we wish to reveal our creative genius to ourselves. Nobody else can know what we are here to do. It cannot be learned in workshops or books or with spiritual teachers. It lives in the cells of your body and it is by listening to those body energies, by listening ultimately to your own heart's desires, that you will discover your story.

When I was about 10 years old, I found an old trunk in the back of a closet I was hiding in to get away from my father's violence. I opened it up and even in the darkness knew that I was looking at my father's lost life, his true self, which was packed away in a hidden treasure chest, hidden primarily from himself.

The chest was filled with beautiful drawings and sketches of women mostly, and some children, as well as soft paintings, which were mostly light reflecting off of different objects, from boats to vases of flowers. I pulled the trunk out of the closet into the light so I could see these very sensitive and lovely bits of my father's soul. The punishment I received for revealing this treasure chest was extreme, as I was opening wounds that he had long ago sealed over, and I was revealing his own lost soul to him.

The intensity of his response was worth it to me, as on some very intuitive level I knew I had uncovered one source of his grief. It was my first glimpse of the profound and very important truth that I was not the cause of his unhappiness. I am sure I had a flicker of compassion for him and for myself that day that set me on a path that saved me from bitterness my whole life.

Going on a treasure hunt for your own lost pieces and shining a light in those dusty corners of your closet can be a fun and exhilarating way to discover new aliveness. Are you hiding your genius from your own awareness? What do you want to uncover and add to your treasure chest? Love will always trump whatever is in your way.

"Dancing with the Starlight Vision"

I open the cells of my being to the life-giving energy of the light of the stars within me.

I am always seeking a new metaphor to play with to help us deepen into our love of ourselves, to remember who we are. Each metaphor gives us a new way to understand our body story and access to the deeper wisdom that the body consistently brings us. There are so many beautiful ways that we can move, using our body wisdom, into the ease of creating our own lives free from all of the personal and cultural conditioning.

We are always in motion if we are alive and we are always spontaneously improvising and creating in every moment. Life is one beautiful sacred improvisation from beginning to end. When we are willing to acknowledge that and live into a constant and ever-evolving state of change, moment by moment, we find ourselves aligned with the divine energy of the universe.

Consciously creating and manifesting these illuminating and deeply nourishing moments of alignment can bring us incredible joy and satisfaction and allow us to bring our sacred gifts to all of those around us and to the earth itself.

Connecting with the light of the stars is one very magical way to remember who you really are, and to deepen your connection to the love that is always flowing into your body. The glowing energy from these celestial beings shines a constant streaming light on you all the time, illuminating all the corners of your goodness.

Gazing down on us, the stars reflect the chemicals and amino acids of our bodies, reminding us of where we came from and that we are actually made of stardust. Every single atom in your body was created in a star billions of years ago. You even have atoms in your body that are over 13 billion years old—very old and very wise atoms.

Stars bless us virtually every night of our lives. They shine their light of unconditional love down through all the layers of our body and all the layers of our consciousness, illuminating our practical knowing, our spiritual journey, and our psychic awareness, all the way down to our pure essence, to our deep divine being, beyond all time, space, and matter.

Let's take a journey together into the shining light of those stars that live both inside us and outside us. You can find an audio guide to this journey online at www.turningthewheel. org/audio.

Begin walking in the room, moving and breathing, and tune into your breath just noticing that you are breathing. Feel your heart beating, 100,000 beats per day, unconditionally loving you, nurturing you, and giving you life. As you are walking and noticing your breath and your heartbeat put your hand on your body and feel your presence under your hand. Try taking a deep breath and placing your hand over your heart, saying, "I am here," a few times, allowing your whole self to arrive in this moment.

Now imagine that you walking outside at night under the stars, in a place where there is no light except the light of the sky. Just keep walking in the room until you find that place, maybe in the high mountains, in the desert, in a meadow, in a forest, at the edge of the ocean or by a lake....

Let yourself go there, into that quiet sacred place and look up into the heavens at your birth place, your ancient beginnings, feeling that direct link to the stars, your body to star body. Move with that starlight, feeling the connection of your body to that beginning, maybe reflecting your gratitude to the stars, dancing your connection, atom to atom.

Move and breathe and sound in this beautiful place you have gone, feeling the gift of illumination the stars are showering down on you, loving you and seeing all of you in the light of their creative power. There is no separation between you and the stars. You are in them and they are in you. As you gaze at them, let yourself feel them gazing back at you.

Become a star looking down on the earth, seeing the waters, always moving and changing directions, finding new ways and possibilities. Notice the patterns of the winds and the birds in the air, and the pathways of the animals making their way across the earth, all the beautiful growing plants and trees, all expressing their particular journey.

See all the human beings negotiating their lives with such striving and commitment, all doing their very best in each moment. And now see your incredibly beautiful illuminated divine being and begin to move and dance and play and connect to this amazing being on the earth—sparkling star to star.

What does your body want to do as it feels bathed and loved by the illumination of the stars? Let your light dance with the light of the stars.

Notice the joy in your soul right now and appreciate yourself for opening up to the never-ending stream of well-being that is always flowing into your body.

Facilitation Suggestions

If you are leading a group, here is one way to slowly bring them back into the room.

Slowly, as you are ready, begin to see the other stars in the room and connect with them with your eyes and your twinkling energy. Notice how your body is responding to being seen by others, and to seeing them.

Maybe you want to play with the other stars in the room, letting your light shine out to them and receiving light back from them.

I would have some sweet and light music here and let your group keep dancing together in joy for a bit. As you see that they are winding down, bring them back together in a circle to sing a joyful song together, like "I Woke Up This Morning" or "I Was on the Rolling Sea"(www.turningthewheel.org/songs), while changing places randomly as they sing, smiling, and celebrating and loving themselves and each other.

As we open up to our own stories and explore loving ourselves more joyfully, we begin to create spontaneous connections with others that are surprisingly deep and lasting. Our bodies know how to do this, how to know self and know other. Every cell in our body is capable of initiating action individually, while communicating with all of the other cells. The more we listen to our bodies and live into their voices of wisdom, the more each of these cells has the chance to express and receive and create with us.

We have been conditioned into an illusion of separateness that can be easily bridged in movement and sound and touch. We don't need to be convinced; we just need to remember that we all belong to each other. The biggest reward there is for falling in love with ourselves is how much love we have to radiate out to others.

The remembering exercise below is an opportunity for your body to experience the sensations of flowing into and out of the molecular field of others, allowing you to experience energetic body-to-body connection and compassion. This experience then becomes a body reference point so you can return here whenever you wish.

"Heart to Heart —Reflection Dance"

I drop gently and quietly into the moving pool of our oneness.

This beautiful group journey is healing and unifying at the same time. It can be a magic pathway to remembering that we are all connected all the time. Loving in isolation is much more challenging. It turns out that happiness is not an individual story. This exercise is a journey designed to give your group the experience of deep and prolonged witnessing that eventually ends in an experience of oneness.

You can use the audio online (www.turningthewheel.org/audio) if you want to participate with your group or use the script below as a guide to leading your group.

Start by finding a new partner. Take a moment to say hello and check in with each other.

One of you is going to move any way your body feels like moving and the other one is going to reflect those movements. Decide who is going to be the mover first and who is going to be the reflector. I will tell you when to switch roles so you can just relax into the exercise.

Stand near each other to start and as you hear the music, take a moment to feel your feet on the floor, relax into your breath, and just allow your energy to drop down into your body, feeling your fluids gently flowing through all of your body.

Mover, move into the space as you are ready, letting the impulses of your body lead and guide you through the space.

Reflector, you get to just drop into a fun and easy space of simply responding to what you see in your mover in any way your body wants to. All of your movements are motivated by what you see your mover doing, though they might look quite different from your mover. You are just reflecting the energy and flow of their body. Let your body guide you and relax into the joy of witnessing the other, body to body.

Beautiful. Try moving around your mover and seeing them from all different angles, noticing parts of their body you may not have witnessed.

Try listening with your whole body to your mover. What happens if you let your stomach or your back or your legs be the listener?

What happens if you let your eyes rest, and see with your heart or your bones?

When you feel the partners have had a chance to explore their role deeply, you can switch the roles.

Now without pausing or speaking, just slowly and gently change roles. If you were the mover begin to shift your focus from yourself to your partner, giving yourself time to transition from that very internal space to the space of reflecting.

If you have been the reflector, begin to move back into your own body, taking time to notice what impulses, sensations and longings are there, letting those lead you into the space.

Mover, as you transition into your own body, just notice your feet on the floor and let your breath be easy, releasing any contractions and drop into the joy of letting your body move effortlessly through the space.

Reflector, now it is your turn to witness your beautiful partner with your body. Let all of your movement be motivated by the flow and energy and shapes and movements of your partner. Just drop in and let your body respond. You are tuning into your mover's molecular story, letting your body stream with their molecules, flowing and blending together.

Let your witness drop into the moment you are in, seeing from moment to moment, breath to breath, moving and breathing from inside your mover.

Allow time for your movers and reflectors to explore the new roles, and deepen even more into their bodies and their connection.

Now keep moving and slowly begin to transition into being both the mover and the reflector, so you are in your own body and responding to your own body while witnessing and responding to your partner's body: looping in and out, "I see you, I see me."

Feel how your fluids mingle and separate and flow in and out of each other, blending and connecting, touching and separating. Let your molecules stream freely. You are just a gathering of molecules, all mingling and flowing together, not really separate from other.

You might have physical contact with your partner, you might go fast or slow, be moving through the room or staying in one place. Just let this duet manifest however it wants to. "This is me, this is you, this is us."

As you are moving together, add in connecting heart to heart, letting all the loving, witnessing energy you have generated stream from your heart to your partner's heart, dancing now from heart to heart.

You might let your eyes connect and feel the loving energy in your heart move into your eyes and stream from your eyes to your partner's eyes and into their heart, receiving love and giving love in an endless loop of well-being.

As you are ready, begin to see others in the room. Let that connection from your heart expand to include others, making eye contact, reflecting back and forth to each other, weaving through the room moving from your heart to their heart and back to yours, remembering to loop back into loving and seeing yourself as you loop out to the room.

All of your molecules are streaming together all the time; all of your molecules are connected to each other and to all the fluids of the earth, the ancient knowing and deep wisdom of those flowing waters—thousands and billions of years old. Feel the ease and joy in being in one big, organic, flowing, moving, energy field: flowing and weaving and dancing together, moving and breathing as one organism.

Facilitation Suggestions

This is another exercise where I pause a lot between cues, giving each member of the group plenty of time to deepen into their own story. I close this by bringing everybody into a circle by just reaching out my hands quietly and letting a circle form up and then do a "Sounding Circle" (p. 281 in the "Resources" section) or a song like "Knowing Love" or "Deep Blue Sea" (www.turningthewheel.org/songs).

I also take time for a small group or partner check in so participants can share how the experience was for them and how they are doing.

Often this is so moving to watch that I am brought to tears. I share with the group the impact their authentic and courageous exploration had on me, and thank them for allowing me to witness such deeply integrated and loving connections.

You can add in other cues, like the ones you see used in the guided journey above, that come up as you witness your group to help them let go of trying or worrying about doing it right. Body cues are the most helpful, so you don't pull participants out of their bodies into thinking about what they are doing.

It helps to keep your cues short and positive like:

"Try witnessing with your eyes closed for a moment."
"Try listening with your spine, as you witness your mover's back."

You may not need to add in any cues. Let your intuition and your unconditional witnessing guide you, letting go of any agenda you may have for the group or anybody in the group. As you are holding and loving the whole room, you get to create an environment where each person is perfect exactly as they are in this moment. Each person will find their own way to their healing and evolution if we just create a clean and open space for them to discover themselves in.

The music is really important here, surrounding and guiding your participants with a gentle and evocative sound. It helps create a feeling of safety, helps the participants go deeper, and makes the whole experience more fulfilling. I feel like Jesse, our musician, co-teaches the class with me through the music he channels into the room.

After the exercise you may want to talk about the reasons for doing this exercise and the benefits of experiencing this kind of connection. You could even divide into smaller groups and let folks share times when the magic of oneness manifested in their lives like the story below.

Drumming on the Mountain

When my fourth child, Norah, was born too early and not expected to live, I had another amazing opportunity to drop into trusting the power of my community and the oneness of our bodies. My mother came and took care of my other children while I stayed at the hospital in Denver with the new baby, keeping my hands on her through the openings in the life support system she was hooked up to. I cried and prayed and sang to her, and kept letting her know that I was there and that she was not alone, looping my energy and love to her. But it did not seem to be enough.

Word of the need for support went out to my whole community very fast as they networked into one web of love and support. This included many people who I would never meet in person, but who linked together to keep the baby alive: my nursing mother friends and their friends, my spiritual group, the parents in the schools that my other children attended, friends in Boulder and other cities, and my family and their friends to name a few.

They all were sending energy and prayers and messages of love to us, and I could feel the power of that energy flowing into my body and into Norah's body.

A few days after she was born, the doctor and nurses said there was nothing more they could do but wait. She was very weak and not responding to treatment and unable to breathe on her own. They did not expect her to live through the night.

That night, my teacher and best friend, the late Eloise Ristad, organized a ritual on the top of Bald Mountain in Boulder and over 50 people came and drummed and chanted all night into the dawn, singing to the baby and sending her their strength and love.

That same night others gathered in their own traditions, including a prayer circle and a meditation group, all sending love and strength to Norah and to me.

Sometime around two in the morning, Norah's body started to completely turn around, and the nurses were literally unhooking machinery all night long as she began to breathe on her own and swallow drops of water. They said they had never seen anything like it and were a little afraid it would slide back again, calling in the doctors to supervise their decisions.

It was truly the stuff of miracles, and the miracle is that we are truly one body of knowing and that there is no separation between us except what we create in our minds. It was the energy and strength of that community of caring and loving folks who actually filled Norah with a life-giving force.

We are actually all deeply connected to everybody and everything on the earth and beyond, and it is from that knowing that we can truly reach out unconditionally in love and compassion.

(A final note: Norah is a very healthy and happy young woman now with a beautiful child of her own, and an incredible career in dance and technology.)

Finding Our True "Yes"

I move into each day filled with gratitude, breathing my own breath, ready for each new beginning.

And so, as we deepen into the loving phase of the healing cycle, we end up back where we started this book, remembering that the real change point is saying "yes" to ourselves on a consistent and reliable basis. And one powerful piece of that "yes" puzzle is sorting out our own story from the stories we have taken on from others.

We are conscious of some of those inherited beliefs about ourselves. We have a good idea of where they came from and can unpack them fairly quickly on the healing cycle. We remember to release to love those times we were shamed, or tried to be good for somebody, or felt inadequate or not smart enough.

Breathing the Mother's Breath

Some of the stories we are living were given to us before we were born, while we were in our mother's body. When you are in the womb you breathe each time your mother breathes, receiving your oxygen directly from her, and you are being imprinted with her patterns of breath, which are tied directly to the quality of her life in that moment. If she is stressed, you are breathing her stress. If she is frightened, you experience the breath of fear, or lack of breath with her, and if she is calm, you receive that calmness.

We also know you share your mother's emotional experiences and that you communicate with her through your senses, which are fully developed by 28 weeks, as are the parts of your brain that connect you to your emotions and to your memory. This can be wonderful. You feel her love for you and her attachment to you. You feel her joy in her successes and her love for your siblings and your father, or simply her enjoyment of the sunset in the evening. You also feel her anger, her longing, her sadness, and her unhappiness.

In short, everything your mother experiences, feels, thinks, and responds to is a very intimate part of your experience as well. If she is still living the life her mother or grandmother longed for, or the life her mother wanted her to live, then she is carrying that legacy forward in her body and handing it down to you.

So the old stories of the generations before are handed down well before your birth, and well before you have choice.

These memories and stories are embedded in your tissues, and I believe one pathway to creating your own true story is to consciously separate from the patterns of your mother's breath and the stories she has handed down body to body.

I remember when I was about 10 years old, my very fundamentalist Christian grandmother came to visit from Southern Illinois. She was very upset that my brothers were drinking beer, that my mother allowed us to play cards, and that we did not pray together as a family. She had a huge fight with my mother and in the course of it was yelling that we would all "burn in hell."

I remember being terrified that I was going to "burn in hell," and not even sure what that meant, but I knew it was bad and it was for bad girls like me.

I saw how stressed and unhappy my mom was and how much she wanted her mother to approve of her and love her. I tried really hard to be good so my grandmother would think my mother had done a good job with me. I was trying to breathe my grandmother's breath for my mother.

But somewhere along the way my mother had begun to breathe her own breath, maybe when she moved to Colorado. And though she felt the pain of failing her mother's vision for how she should live her life, she had begun to find her way into a different story that was at least closer to her own.

Every time she let go of one more of the pieces of her great-grandmother's, grandmother's, and mother's scripts, she also released me from pieces of those stories. As you turn lovingly and gently towards those old stories, both the ones that work for you and the ones that don't, you help free the next generation to breathe their own breath.

The members of that next generation will need to find their own stories as well. If you have released yourself from the generational stories you took on, then you will happily and consciously collaborate with them in releasing the stories they inherited from your path.

The Premiere

I had a very dramatic experience of this with my very intuitive and brilliant daughter, Andrea, when I staged my first fully produced, full-length evening show, which interestingly enough was titled "The Awakenings." She was in college in the east at the time and flew out to the opening of the show, knowing that my stepping publicly into to my powers as an artist was significant for her life as well.

She came to me the morning after the premiere, asking me what was happening inside me, saying she had woken up feeling released and shifted in her energy, and that it felt connected to me and to the performance. Andrea knew that she had been released from an old story of oppression and victimhood I had been carrying forward.

I had definitely walked through a portal the night before with a sold-out house and standing ovations for my first show, and a totally new sense of who I was and the impact I could have on the earth. I had decided to manifest my own essence.

My mom gave up all her personal dreams to serve her children and her husband, as did my grandmother. I knew that I had broken a pattern for all of our family that night, and Andrea had directly felt the impact. A new story had just become conscious for me and for my children.

"Letting Go of the Mother's Breath—Becoming Breathtaking!"

The very good news is that we all can access these patterns through movement and breath and put them consciously on the healing cycle. As you release your mother's breath, you literally become "breathtaking" -- taking new and full breaths that belong only to you. And that, in turn, takes you to falling even more passionately and enthusiastically in love with yourself.

In the journey below, we will both thank our mother for the gifts she gave us and give her back pieces we no longer need, pieces that do not serve us anymore. You can do this alone, but because it is a deep dive, I suggest doing it with a friend if you are not part of a guided group exploration.

Let's begin with writing the "Mother's Breath" exercise (you'll find it on p. 272 in the "Resources" section). Take a moment to find your pen and your copy of the exercise, and find a place in the room to begin writing.

We will write for 20 minutes. (If you are doing this exercise on your own, set a gentle sounding timer so you will know when to stop.) Just fill in the sentence stems with your own answers. You could spend your whole time writing any one of these sentence stems or answer them all with only a few words or skip any that do not resonate for you.

As you are writing, keep changing your position a little or a lot. You could write lying on your back or belly or walking around the room or with your paper up on the wall, or you could just uncross your legs or change the direction you are facing. I will remind you to change your position a couple of times in the next 20 minutes.

Let's begin together. Close you eyes for a moment and notice any places in your body that need to release or relax a little, and send those places some warm loving energy and support.

Now move around a little and take a deep breath and wiggle a little until you feel present. Begin writing as you are ready.

When you are complete, find a partner who is also done, and share whatever you feel comfortable sharing, while giving and receiving some support. Sometimes you get more ideas of what you would like to give back to your mother from your partner, as our stories are always so similar, despite different characters in the roles.

"I Give You Back"

Writing this exercise takes us all the way through the healing cycle in words. We get present and experience some discovery, some awakening to our own ancestry. Out of that we begin the natural process of embracing our history as we uncover some of the pieces of the puzzle that create our patterns of separation in our world.

Loving that history and appreciating the people who were part of our growing years and the gifts they gave us allows us to also give them back whatever we don't want to carry forward. This step opens the door for reclaiming parts of ourselves that were underneath other stories and to have a sense of renewed empowerment in our ability to create our own journey forward.

Finally, we feel the release from those scripts and ways of being that do not belong to us as we begin to create new actions for our new beginning, breathing our own breath and gently reaching with empowered joy into our own future.

In this next step of the exercise we will experience in our bodies that place of loving and acting, so our cells and brain and bones and fluids can align with our new story. The online recording (www.turningthewheel.org/audio) will guide you through this if you are doing it by yourself or with a friend.

Stand facing the past, wherever that seems to be for your body right now. Take a moment to feel your feet firmly on the ground, and notice that you are breathing. Close your eyes and pause a moment, placing your hand on your heart. Say out loud to yourself "I am here," letting your hand move gently down the front of your body. Do this three times.

As you are ready, blink open your eyes and take a step forward and say "I am here" again, and take a deep breath.

I appreciate....

Now see your mother across the room from you, or feel her energy there, and tell her that you love her and begin a dance of words and movement, telling her all the things you appreciate about her and the gifts she gave you.

You might appreciate her gardening skills that taught you how to grow beautiful flowers, or her ability to create order in the house, or the beautiful perfume bottles on her dresser. Speak these appreciations, sing them, dance them, move them, throw them to the heavens, whisper them, and body drum them. Run around the room as you thank her, or stand beside her and surround her energy with your loving gratitude.

When you feel complete, come to stillness and just notice your body and your breath and ground back into this moment. Come back to "I am here," and appreciate yourself for your generous sharing and for your capacity to love.

I give you back....

As you take another deep breath, see your mother again across the room or feel her energy there, and tell her that you have some things you want to return to her as you move forward in your life.

You might want to give her back her fear of not being enough, or not having enough, or her belief that others were responsible for her happiness, or her hatred of her body or her drinking habits or repressed sexuality. Using the paper you wrote just keep giving back anything you don't want to take forward with you anymore.

Continue talking directly to her, moving and sounding in any way you want as you tell her all the things you wish to return.

I give you back….

Say each phrase more than once. You might speak quietly or boldly. Try emphasizing different words in your "I give you back…" phrase. Try different tones of voice. Do you feel calm or emphatic, centered or agitated, sad or relieved, angry or frustrated? Move different ways as you speak, reflecting how you are feeling, clearing and cleaning your psyche, making room for your own soul's journey.

When you are complete, take a moment and come back to stillness and hold and hug yourself, and appreciate your courage and your commitment to evolving and growing as a conscious human being.

Now make your way back to your partner and share your experience with them, deepening your connection, as you unconditionally witness each other and honor your partner's integrity and body knowing with your affirmative listening. Your "yes" to them is expressed in the good attention you are giving them, releasing them from the old story of needing to be fixed.

"That Was Then, This Is Now"

Thank your partner and move out into the room, walking and breathing and coming into your own body, feeling your feet on the ground. We are going to complete this exploration with a simple pointing and speaking exercise.

As you are walking, pause when you feel the impulse and with your left hand point in the direction that feels like the past to you in this moment and say, "That was then," and then put your right hand on your heart and say "This is now."

Just keep doing this over and over—walking, pausing, and pointing in whatever direction seems right as you say the words "That was then," and putting your other hand on your heart and saying, "This is now."

Now have fun varying how you're a saying the words and how you are moving while you say them. You might sing them, drum them on your legs, say them over and over really quickly, or say them very emphatically, gently or laughingly.

Keep going and now just change the words to "That was you, This is me," using the same hand gestures, one for pointing and one for bringing yourself home to your own body in this moment.

As you are walking through the room make your way to your partner and check in and share one last time.

Get a drink of water if you wish and find your pen and notebook. Sit quietly for a few minutes to let all you have just experienced have a chance to land and integrate a little. Then when you are ready, take the next 10 minutes to write down what you want to remember from this exercise, or what you learned or just write what is coming up for you right now.

Be sure to take care of yourself after taking this journey, maybe a nice warm bath, sitting quietly in nature, a cup of warm tea, or a long walk with a friend. As all of this keeps bubbling in your psyche, remember to love yourself and all the little voices that need attention. Ask for any support you need to stay present in the process and move through to a new place.

(Thanks to Katie Hendricks for "That Was Then, This Is Now.")

Facilitation Suggestions

As a facilitator, you have the honor of witnessing these courageous participants and surrounding them with love and with respect for their integrity and willingness to keep evolving. You can keep looping out with love for them and then looping in with love for yourself.

Keep breathing, trusting the health and strength of each participant. If someone seems to be really struggling at any point, you can give them support by placing your hand in the middle of their back and applying a little pressure, "backing them up," and if necessary remind them to feel their feet on the ground.

Step IV
Acting
Acting, Allowing, Releasing

Affirmation: I am ready to align with my essence and move with ease and joy in my life while manifesting my sacred gifts.

The final step on the healing cycle, creating and manifesting your action, is your reward for the amazing journey of evolution you have just taken around the mandala. You know you have an action step when you have chosen something you can actually do and be able to tell that you have done it. This usually means finding an achievable starting point and then building on that. Your enthusiasm will build step by step as each action step is completed.

The key is to make your commitment, your action step, in a co-creative partnership with the loving source, knowing that with every shift you make into trust and love, the entire collective unconscious shifts with you, allowing your change to vibrate out to the whole world. You become the source, a channel for healing to come into the world.

What is so exciting is that you are re-patterning your brain into new possibilities with these simple, loving action steps. Simply align yourself with your intentions and you are free to manifest what you want right now—connection by connection. The brain loves spontaneity, new possibilities, change, and evolution, and it is always standing by to do your bidding.

Though it will be up to you to manifest your own true story, it helps to have a partner to witness your action steps. Because you have moved through the step of loving, you are ready to be seen by others in your authentic self, and being lovingly seen is one of the keys to manifesting more easily and effortlessly.

Your story can get caught in resisting instead of creating. Freedom really comes from moving into what you want, and who you are with a clear mind and proactive movement.

Phrases like "I am not...," "I will not...," or "I am done with...," are most likely paths into old stories of anger and victimhood. These phrases have to do with some way you took on another person's attempt to control you and to which you still respond.

Maximum Freedom

Maximum freedom comes from moving clearly into asking, "What do I want right now?" Then we get to let go of any outcome, timing, or idea of how it might come to be, and just allow it to happen. We come face to face with the paradox of taking clear actions towards living our own true story and releasing outcomes at the same time. To truly be empowered, we live into the beautiful paradox of landing clearly and happily where we are and letting go in trust.

To truly surrender to this trust we need to develop a body comfort with not knowing—with living in the moment and with letting the next step present itself. This is a vulnerable and very alive way to live your true story.

To trust this deeply, we must maintain a practice of loving and appreciating ourselves, all of who we are and all of what we bring. If we had been raised believing that we were always being held and nurtured in the arms of the Great Mother or unconditionally loved by the Great Spirit, we would probably carry this feeling unconsciously with us all the time.

So here is a practice, an action step, to deepen consciously into that appreciation and step into an empowered future. This can be done each morning before you put your feet on the earth and activate your day's story, or just before you fall asleep at night. It is gentle and your body and soul will love it. If you are doing this alone, putting on some meditative music can be supportive and create a container for you.

Rocking in the Arms of Love

Lie on the floor on your back and place your arms on your chest crossing each other. Just lay them gently there and begin by feeling their presence. Focus on your hands and let them send you loving energy—right down into your heart space. As you begin to feel that energy radiating into your body, let yourself be aware of something that you know is beautiful about you, something that is deeply good about your essence. Just let a thought float up into your consciousness, and be there with that energy.

Take a breath and feel the Great Spirit holding you in her arms and rocking you back and forth. Maybe you hear her singing a soft chant to you. You might even sing or sound out loud to yourself. Your body loves the sound of your own voice.

As you are being rocked let your awareness float to all the ways you have loved and served in this life already, ways you have given to others from your own strengths and gifts.

Notice all the little ways you show up in your life for others and see possibilities for them, and the ways you love those around you and the earth, the animals, the waters, the trees, the sky, the stars…

Now let your awareness float to all the ways you have received and accepted love in your life, all the ways you have let others into your heart. Notice the love that is there for you in your life right now and let it flow gently into your cells and move through your whole body, infusing your essence through your fluids.

Come back now to feeling the strong arms that are cradling you and rocking you and let yourself rest into that rocking, just letting go and resting deeply into the safety of those arms.

As you slowly bring your awareness back into the room, move your body gently, rocking yourself up to sitting, and just notice how your body feels. You may want to move for a few moments to the music that is playing, or in silence, to help your body integrate what you have just done. Let your body move however it wants to move until you feel a sense of completion or landing.

(Inspired by Angeles Arrien.)

Facilitation Suggestions

If you are guiding a group you can take them into connection with each other by following the script below. You can find the audio version online (www.turningthewheel.org/audio).

As you are ready, begin to see others in the room and connect a little with your eyes or your energy, just noticing how that is for you.

As the music begins to play, let your body move however it wants to move to the sacred music you are hearing. You might move a little or a lot, stay slow or maybe begin to move a little faster. Maybe you will play with someone else if you are in a group, or maybe just stay on your own. Take your time to find your way back into the room in your own way.

As you become more and more awake to the room, let yourself find a partner and play back and forth with giving and receiving energy and weight, giving and receiving support. Notice how it feels to interact from a place of having truly appreciated yourself.

Try a little dance of joy with your partner, feel the love moving back and forth between you.

Take a moment to appreciate yourself for showing up in your own life and committing to manifesting your own true story.

The great and beautiful sea of all living beings thanks you too.

Facilitation Suggestions
After the group has had a chance to play with their partner I would guide them into another round of "This Is Me, This Is You" (p. 111) to close the exploration. Then they could share with that partner for a few minutes before moving on.

Two-Footedness

Standing in Our Intentions

I step with all my energy into a place of balance in my life where my deep longing is allowed to flow out—planting seeds of love.

Once we have begun to breathe our own breath and move and breathe in our own fluid body, taking our cues from our body sensations, we discover a wonderful feeling that we call "two-footedness." It is an exhilarating state of feeling yourself in complete alignment with your intention in that moment, and it seems almost mystical at first.

Because you have been through the healing cycle—awakening, embracing, and loving, you are ready to feel your own two-footed "yes" to your action steps through your whole body, knowing you can create the future you want right now. As you land on two feet, you feel your movement and voice and body align with what you know in your heart and you come into a fully embodied "yes."

In many traditions this is more simply called whole heartedness, where you tune into your heart and see if it is open and freely flowing into an aligned two-footed moment. If any place is resisting even a little, it is good to love that place and to put it on the healing cycle and clear it before completing your process.

Unfortunately, we spend much of our time in our lives straddling between many places at once, moving rapidly from one foot to the other without a pause as we rush between different places, playing many different roles, trying to do our best in each one. Culturally we have been conditioned to be all things to all people and this one-footed story often leads to living in a state of unconscious stress, turning quickly away from our own needs or longings.

We even pretend to be fully two-footed at times to please ourselves or others. We playfully call this "faking two-footedness," and it is extremely stressful at best. This happens a lot when we stay in jobs or marriages, for example, that we are unhappy in.

Paradoxically, there are times when we need to be on one foot, slightly off balance and considering all options, and standing without stress in not knowing. We call this a "two-footed maybe," where we are clear that it is time to pause and to let something arise from a place we haven't been before, or a place we don't remember. Once you are comfortable negotiating being a little off balance as you explore options, and comfortable giving your body wisdom time to speak, you will be able to trust that you will know when to land with both feet planted firmly on the ground.

"Landing with Two Feet"

This action step is a way to land two-footed in your body and a way to explore all the choices and variations around that. It is a good way to get comfortable with the chaos and impermanence of life in today's world and a fun way to flush out your system and come back into balance in your life.

You can easily do it alone after reading through the group exercise below, or you can have a lot of fun doing it in any group.

Begin with feeling both of your feet solidly on the ground and placing your hand on your heart as you speak "I am here." Rock back and forth from one foot to the other, letting your balance stabilize through the movement. Speak "I am here" as you begin to step slowly into the room, finding the strength of your presence and clarity. Let your body be loose, feeling the fluids streaming and moving all through your body, giving you flexibility and readiness.

Slowly speed up a little and when you feel an impulse to land, pause and step firmly into your two-footed stance. Breathe there for a moment and then move out into the room again, pausing a few more times to land firmly on your two feet and just notice how that feels for you.

Now play with being off balance, moving rapidly from foot to foot, and place to place, letting yourself fall forwards and then backwards and then sideways as you quickly move from one place to another. Change directions frequently, shifting your focus all the time from one part of the room to another, and catching yourself before you actually fall.

I demonstrate this as I speak the instructions, showing how it looks in my body rapidly falling and rushing from one foot to another. I often also add in a monologue like the one below. (You are likely to have your own version.) It is fun and more than a little addictive, though ultimately exhausting.

The monologue might go something like this:

"I am getting the groceries and taking this phone call and checking to see if I have enough money, while worrying about the time as I load the groceries while talking on the phone. I head out to pick up my boy at school, knowing I am late and wondering if I got what he

needs for his lunch tomorrow. On the way home, while I am asking him how his day was, we stop to drop off some things to a friend and then get one more grocery item I forgot while I am calling back the doctor to confirm my appointment." And so it goes.

OK everybody begin, add in words if you choose. Push the limits as far as you are comfortable—really letting yourself feel the sensation of being off balance. Notice how it feels to be off balance.

Now jump into your two-footed stance again and pause. Drop into your breath, letting your whole energy field land right there in that moment. Relax into the stillness, and notice how your feel in your body. Notice your breath and your heart rate, and allow your whole being to come to quiet. How does it feel to be landed?

From here move to each place in the room again, quickly if you wish, even being off balance along the way, and then land in each place on both your feet, and then to the next place, fully inhabiting each stop even if just for a moment. You could even say at each one "I am here."

Now go back and forth between the two, rushing about with no two-footed landings and then land in some two-footed pauses again, giving your body the experience and the information.

As you close this exploration, try moving in ways that please you and nourish you, creating an easy two-footed body experience of moving in alignment with your body. Notice the power of that alignment, vibrating all through your cells.

Slowly dance your way to a partner and take a few minutes to move and play together and then share how that was for you and how you are feeling right now.

"A Tiny Bit of Support"

Because we often have too much on our plates and often find ourselves rushing about, there is another strategy I like to play with in our bodies, which is to get some support when we need it, to ask for help. As we know, our very survival depends on understanding our interdependence with each other and with the earth.

Our reluctance to ask for support, once again, is rooted in our belief that we are separate from one another and that we "need to take care of ourselves and our own responsibilities, and not inconvenience others."

This very modern view of the earth and its inhabitants only increases the chaos that we all live in and creates a system of isolation and often despair that is painful and that perpetuates itself. From this place we often begin to blame someone else—or other cultures or other countries—for our unhappiness.

What is surprising is that we often only need a little bit of help or support to feel fully stable and strong again. It is easier to pause and a wait for answers to arise if we have some help and support in the interim. As we drop into connection, we find those easy, beautiful connection points that will ultimately support easy, beautiful forward motion.

This time begin playing a little more gently in the space with off balance and on balance, moving through the space from one foot to the other and tipping yourself off balance a little as you go. Every now and then reach out and put a hand on someone's shoulder for balance—just lightly.

Notice how little support you actually need to restore your balance or notice how much of a difference giving just a little support makes for someone else.

Maybe you will reach your hand out to offer some support to someone else, allowing them to restore their balance, or reach your hand out asking for a hand. Play with all the ways you can connect lightly with each other as you move through the room giving and receiving little bits of loving care.

Now add in all the pieces to explore and play with together. Feel yourself reeling through space, barely keeping upright, and then rooted firmly with two feet on the ground, then supporting a friend, or letting yourself receive some support. Have fun in this dance of authentic connection.

"Finding a Fit"

Sometimes all of the movement and visualizing and imagining just won't land in a two-footed, usable action step for you or for your participant. I use the "Finding a Fit" worksheet (on p. 265 in the "Resources" section) to help focus and gather information in a different way. It can feel like an amazing and very simple miracle.

What do I want?

What is needed that I can give?

How do these two go together?

You can just free write these questions on your own and see what bubbles up that surprises you. Then you could use the healing cycle to move around through embracing and loving and acting. You could do the exercise with a friend as well and deepen your connection to your friend as you deepen your connection to yourself. The script below can be a guide if you wish to use this with a group.

When you have found your copy of the "Finding a Fit" worksheet, find a partner to work with, and then find a place in the room for the two of you to get comfortable. Decide who is going first. The first speaker will spend four minutes answering the question "What do I want?" in any way he or she wants. I will tell you when the four minutes is up.

Listener, you will be the scribe for the speaker, trusting that you will catch what is important. Just write single words and phrases so the speaker can let thoughts flow out. Be sure to pause and make eye contact with your speaker and loop loving attention to them and to yourself.

If your speaker needs encouraging you can use simple prompts, like "What else do you want?" or "Tell me more about that." Your job is to listen with the intent to encourage, letting your whole body say, "yes."

All right, that was four minutes.

Speaker, go ahead and finish your sentence or your thought and then pause.

Listener, take a minute and respond in movement to what you have just witnessed. Let your body speak through movement and affirm and appreciate all that your partner has revealed and shared with you.

Speaker, allow yourself to be blessed and take in this beautiful reflection of your words.

Now change roles. The speaker will become the listener for four minutes.

Guide your group through the other two questions in the same way. When you are complete, have the partners join with another set of partners so they are in groups of four and let them share what they discovered.

Facilitation Suggestions

One of our workshop participants came up to me when I presented this exercise and said the whole reason I am here is because I do not know what I want, so how can I write about it. It was such a good question and so courageous of her to come up and speak it out loud to me. That was my first clue that she did, as we all do, know quite a lot about what she wanted. First she wanted to come and talk to me and tell me that she didn't know, and she did that—already a significant thread of health emerging.

So we began to break down the question together. The following suggestions can help if you or one of your participants is feeling stuck or even frightened by the whole idea of asking for what they want.

Did she want anything different in her relationships with others?
Did she want anything different around her financial situation?
Did she want any changes with her relationship to food or her body?
Did she want to travel anywhere?
What did she love to do most with her time and did she want to do more of that?
What had she done in the last month that was inspiring or fulfilling?

We also went back to the "Journey to Joy" exercise (see p. 266 in the "Resources" section), another great tool for seeking our passion. We moved and played with the questions in that exercise that had energy for her. After a short 20 minutes, she had a list of what she wanted that was so long, the problem was where to begin.

When we took that list and moved on to the second question of "What is needed that I can give?" her list began to focus and sort itself out. One of the things she wanted was to feel like she mattered to somebody, like she was important. So we could immediately plug some of her desires into what is needed in her community and we were off.

I had a beautiful email from her a few months later where she shared that she had gone through a few different iterations and ultimately landed working with differently-abled adults, using the exercises in our book, *Dancing Our Way Home,* combined with all of her joyful creativity and fine arts background to enrich their lives and her life every day.

"Build a Seed"

A few of years ago at our summer retreat I realized that a group game we had been playing with kids all over the country was a perfect way to embody this issue of finding a fit, especially if it is done really slowly with beautiful music that helps us drop into a contemplative internal space. Since then we have used this very simple form over and over as an easy way to practice seeing and then acting in our bodies.

Facilitation Suggestions

If you have played the "Running Seeds" game (p. 102), with your group, then this will only take a few minutes to set up and demonstrate.

Begin by dividing your group into smaller groups of four or five. I usually have someone demonstrating as I talk. If you don't have a team with you, choose someone to start that you know is comfortable with movement and then you can be the one to demonstrate how the second person would join in.

This game is a variation of the "Running Seeds" that is quiet and contemplative and very slowed down so you can drop into the center of your beautiful being.

One person from your group will begin by stepping out into the space around your group, and taking their time, moving and breathing, they will find the shape that will start your seed. John will start for us.

When he is still, the next person (another volunteer) will go out. She gets to take all the time she wants, noticing what seems to be calling to her from the shape that is there, while also listening to what her body wants to do in this moment. What do I want and what is needed and how do they fit together? Beautiful.

Now the next person will go. Remember to take all the time you want as you begin this. There is no hurry and this is a chance to drop all the way in and manifest from your body knowing. As each person takes a turn, the witnesses get to practice looping loving energy to the seeker.

OK. Find a space in the room for your group and join hands for a moment, feeling your connection and caring for each other. Begin when you are ready, as one of you starts the exploration.

"Connect the Dots"

This is another slightly more conscious group exercise than "Finding a Fit" that plays with making a choice in each moment about who you want to align yourself with in the room and ultimately, as the exercise progresses, deciding if you want to stand independently and bring a new story into the room, that is if you want to be an innovator in that moment.

This exercise allows your participants to have a direct body experience of an awareness that is needed in our lives every day. Am I consciously supporting the status quo in a way that is in alignment with my values and do I want to do that, or do I want to bring in a new idea? It can be challenging as it has choice and spontaneity mixed together, and that choice also adds in awareness of community. It is important to remember that innovation is a "yes, and."

We will begin by spreading out in the room and finding a spot standing on the floor that is your spot or your dot. We are going to connect these dots with our bodies, instead of with a pencil. Does everybody have a spot?

OK. When I say go, everyone will go to one of the dots that have already been established in the room. More than one person can end up on the same dot. So you will leave your dot, or spot on the floor, and go to another existing one and pause there. Just look around and let your body move to your new place when I say go.

Go.

Do that one more time.

Go.

Great.

Now you will cue this movement internally, so when anybody moves, everybody will move, and then all stay still until somebody moves again. See if you can all move at the same time and come to stillness at the same time.

Let this continue for a few minutes so the participants get the rhythm of moving and coming to stillness together.

Pause. That was great, really good awareness of each other. Give yourselves a hand! (Clapping)

Let's reset now and find a new spot in the room to begin again. This time take a shape on your spot—any shape you want. It can be big or little, something you do every day like pointing or crossing your arms, or something you have never done before, or something that feels fun or dancer-like, or a little crazy. It is all good.

The more you do what feels good to you in the moment, the more fun the game is for you and for everyone. Here we go. Take your shape and hold it. Now when anybody moves everybody moves to a new dot and takes the shape of the person that was on that dot. Again, more than one person can be on a dot taking the same shape. And you can only take a shape that already exists in the room.

Let this go on for a while. It is really fun to do and to watch. Soon the shapes will become fewer and fewer and everyone could even end up in one or two shapes as the game progresses. When that happens, or before if it is going on too long, have the participants reset for the third step.

OK pause here for a moment. That was incredible to watch – so authentic and interesting with all the varied shapes and the beautiful awareness of each other, really creating community. Give yourselves a hand again.

Before we do the final step, take a moment and turn to someone near you and each take a turn appreciating yourself, if nothing else for how much you showed up and co-created this moment together.

Let's reset one more time, so find a spot in the room that is your starting point and get ready to take a shape.

This time you can either go to a dot and a shape that exists in the room or you can start a new spot and take a new shape. You get to decide each time if you want to help sustain what is traditional or grounding this group, or whether you want to bring in a new idea that might move this community forward.

Do you want to be an innovator in this moment or a sustainer?

Begin. You are still all moving at the same time and coming to stillness at the same time as you explore this new idea.

Let yourself play back and forth, trying out being the innovator and trying out being the one who holds the ground. Notice what feels best to you. Have fun and experiment, maybe making a shape you have never made before.

Both of these roles are important and both are needed. This is about collaborating and noticing what is needed in the moment. If everyone brings in a new shape all the time we would never have any cohesiveness or maybe even safety. If we never bring in new ideas, we get stuck and stale in our stories and in our way of viewing the world.

This is so amazing to witness. Keep going and now you can move or be still on your own time, taking shapes you see or introducing new shapes, being still or moving when your own body impulses speak to you.

You will need a music change here if you do not have a musician following your group.

Keep going and let go of all instructions and just see each other and play and move together in the space, expressing you own energy and your gratitude for this amazing open and willing group who came to play with you today.

Facilitation Suggestions

We created this form during the rehearsals for one of our big touring performances, and it has turned out to be a standard in our teaching. It is an easy and fun way to get your group connected and into a state of "yes." And it is really exquisite to watch, so this is a good one to remember if you are staging a community performance.

It is also a beautiful mirror of what happens in our communities and in businesses and families. We have a ground, a base that is established and needed to keep order and have some small illusion of predictability in our lives. And, at the same time, we can only advance as a civilization by honoring the new and opening up to new ways all the time. This is a great way for your group to explore their preferences around that and to find ways to support those differences in each other.

"Planting Joy"

Twenty-five years ago, when I was at a turning point of my life, Thich Nhat Hanh, a Zen Master, global spiritual leader, poet and peace activist, gave me this beautiful way to view my path. I remember him asking the group if we were "planting seeds of happiness in our garden." It was the first time I really landed in the awareness that my own garden was as important as all the gardens around me that I was watering so diligently.

Planting in my garden is a metaphor and an action step for well-being that I come back to over and over, seeing my body and my soul as a garden that I am planting and nurturing with many different kinds of seeds. The questions I ask myself are: Am I planting and watering seeds of joy, and of love? What am I cultivating, and what do I want to grow in my garden?

Thich Nhat Hanh made it very simple for us. If you plant beans, beans will grow, if you plant joy, joy will grow, if you plant and water anger, anger will grow. This was so important for me as I realized I was still watering some old anger from my childhood that I didn't want to nurture anymore, and that I could focus on planting and nurturing what I wanted, instead of what I didn't want. It is all there and part of the shaman's pot of wisdom. And it all informs our compassion and knowing. The choice is what to strengthen and support.

If we reach for the seeds in our life that are healing and bring us joy, they will bloom a new reality into our souls, and the suffering will fall away. Everything can be transformed by love, and if we keep watering that love for ourselves and for all others and for the earth, transformation happens without our even knowing it, effortlessly.

The following journey into your garden is one gift that grew in my garden as I turned towards ease and health. You can do this alone, using the audio recording (www. turningthewheel.org/audio), and then use the script below with your own beautiful images to lead a group through the exercise together.

Before we begin, place your journal and pen in a spot where you can easily find it at the end of our journey.

Begin by simply walking and breathing in the room and noticing any place in your body that needs a little love or warmth or releasing. Make some sounds if that helps you get present, find your hum again, feel your feet on the floor, and just relax into the moment.

We are first going to bloom the being inside you, your very own secret garden. Let your awareness drop down to your pelvic floor, a fertile place to begin your garden. Imagine a beautiful red flower beginning to bloom there, opening up into your abdomen and becoming many blooms as it fills your whole abdomen and naval area with fragrant flowers.

See those blooms multiplying and opening in many different colors as they keep filling your whole inner landscape—up through your belly, gently curling around your spine and into your chest, surrounding your lungs and your heart, and up behind your eyes.

Let your heart open to the beauty of who you are, expanding into the immensity of your capacity to grow and bloom love.

Let your body expand and grow bigger and more spacious, making more and more room for these amazing blooming beings. Maybe they grow down your arms into your fingers and down your legs into your toes.

Let your body dance their dance and sing their song as they fill your whole body, your heart and your soul with the confidence and love of their healing energy.

After a few moments say:

As you are moving and sounding through the room, let this garden begin to manifest around you in the room. Now you are moving through your garden, dancing in among the trees and flowers and grasses.

Keep moving around this garden and see what is here, maybe a stream or a fountain, maybe some purple iris, or yellow daisies, some ferns and moss along the path.

Are there ponds with lilies and fish, or places to sit? Wildflowers may be growing along the edges of this abundant and full garden.

Take your time and create your garden, looking to the right and left and right down by your feet.

After a few moments say:

What are the sounds in this garden? Do you hear birds singing, a breeze quietly blowing, bees humming, or chattering squirrels? Maybe you can hear the growing plants as they bloom possibilities for abundance and well-being in your life.

Maybe you want to dance with the trees and grasses and play in your garden, talking and singing with the animals and blooms.

Maybe there is a place where you want to sit for a while or lie down on the earth where you can smell the smells and rest in the peace and quiet of your beautiful garden.

Take another walk around your garden as you come back into the room, bringing the sensations in your body from the garden back with you.

Make your way to your journal and write or draw this garden. You might record how you are feeling as you experience your inner landscape blooming and tumbling out into the world in all of its beauty.

Now make groups of four and share your gardens and your blooming with each other.

Facilitation Suggestions
Once again, live music or really deep and beautiful spirit music is important here to help your participants take the journey into their garden.

I go very slowly with this, creating long enough pauses between speaking for the images to arise and expand.

"May I, May You"

This is one of my favorite action steps, and a wonderful place to finish the "Acting" section on the "The Body Now" mandala. "May I, May You" deepens your connection with your partner while deepening your connection to your own self-love. It is a very kind and tender way to affirm each other and to ground yourself into your own intentions.

This works well as a closing to almost any class.

Find a partner and find a place in the room where you would like to stand and face each other. You will take turns asking for what you want in a simple, repetitive form. Decide who will go first.

Then the first person will ask for what they want to manifest in their life by saying, for example, "May I—see my grandchildren more often."

The listener will then say back to the speaker exactly what they said like this, "May you—see your grandchildren more often."

Then the listener will ask, for example, "May I—make more time for sleep in my life." And the new listener will say to the speaker exactly what they said like this, "May you—make more time for sleep in your life,"

So you simply change the pronoun to you or your, and keep everything else the same, with no added suggestions or embellishments, though it can be tempting.

For example, one could respond to the person who asked to get more sleep in their life like this "May you get smart about your health and make it a priority to get more sleep no matter what." This is an exaggeration, but not as far off as one might think. This exercise is another opportunity to reflect and accept the other person in unconditional love, and to just let the fixing and advising go!

So you just alternate back and forth, each taking a turn to ask and to reflect and feel yourself falling in love with this person as you truly see them and feel them seeing you back.

Facilitation Suggestions

I let this go on for a while as it deepens as it goes. It is such a non-threatening way to ask for what you want and to be seen. You can tell by watching your group when they have had enough.

Reclaiming Our Path

I step courageously into the forest of my interior self, and begin the journey to my own true story, to my essence.

This last section of the book is a magical journey into the mysteries of authenticity and self-love all rolled together into one long sequence that could be a weekend workshop, a six-week evening empowerment class, or spread out over a week-long retreat. It is a little deeper dive when taken all together, and it is designed for a facilitator to be a guide for others along the way. It will keep your group moving around "The Body Now" mandala in an elegant and creative pathway.

You could also pull any of these exercises out of this sequence and use them on their own, weaving them into something else you are doing with a different theme or time line. Once you have read through this section, and tried some of the exercises yourself with the audio aids available online (www.turningthewheel.org/audio), you will know how you want to integrate them into your own work with others.

The journeys we are assigned to live by our families, our parents and grandparents, our churches, our schools, our neighborhoods, and our peers, by the prevailing myths and belief systems in the countries and cultures we live in, and even by our ancestry, belong to the people or organizations that gave them to us. Rarely do they take us to our own authentic gifts, or to a life filled with the kind of alignment and fulfillment that we are all seeking.

Luckily, we can give these stories back, and appreciate all the good things we learned while we were on that path. There are always gifts along the way: skills and wisdom that we can take forward on our own true journey.

And the good news is that woven all through that assigned pathway are bits and pieces of our own unique magic, emerging and showing up along the way. Your unique, amazing self has always been there and will always be there. And you can create a path that carries you forward into those authentic and magical parts of your amazing self, reclaiming pieces you left behind and discovering new ways of being along the way. Which path will carry you to the realm of pure delight and radical spontaneity?

Below you will find a complete journey out of the past and into the present with all possibilities restored to you and to your participants. It is a journey around the healing cycle into manifesting your true self in joy and celebration.

Facilitation Suggestions

A good way to begin this journey is to warm your group up with "Spaces Between" before you start (p. 285 in the "Resources" section). This helps the participants get fully embodied and creates an expansive, open energy. If you are doing this over several days, it is important to do movement games and exercises each time to help your participants get present and relaxed in their bodies. This creates physical as well as emotional safety for your group.

A Journey to the Forest

Before we chart our path forward we are going to do three wonderful discovery exercises to gather information for the journey and reclaim some pieces that we will need along the way. If this were a fairy tale, and you were seeking the secret to your life's purpose, you would go deep into the forest to the hut of Baba Yaga, the wise old witch, and ask her to tell you the secret.

As the story goes, she would give you three tasks to perform and command you to return to her hut only when you had completed those tasks with proof that you had completed them. Then, and only then, would she would reveal the secret of your life's purpose to you.

So here we go—our three tasks.

Task 1: "Walking the Past"

Our first task is to walk the path of what has come before and see what we learn and what we want to take forward with us as our proof for Baba Yaga that we have done the task.

You first need to get a pen and a notebook that you can carry with you and draw on as you walk through the room.

Begin by finding a place in the room that is your starting point. It doesn't matter where as long as it feels right to you.

This is not a linear timeline where you record each event and write about it—although that can also be a good exercise to do. This is a stream of consciousness line, moving across and around your page or pages as your hand responds to the journey you are walking and narrating out loud as you walk.

The whole journey may be a spiral for you, spiraling in or spiraling out. It may begin as a line and turn into many concentric circles, double back on itself many times, be accented with dots or squiggles, have spikes of high and low, be a big overlapping mass, a tidy little set of lines, or anything else that comes into your hand.

Just begin walking and thinking about your experiences, maybe specific events, and all of the people along the way, starting at whatever age has energy for you and let you hand record the journey. While you are walking and drawing, you can talk or sing or mumble or sound along the way if you wish.

If you are leading others in this exercise, pause and demonstrate here, using your own life, walking and drawing and talking out loud so they can see how it works.

We will do this for a while, so take your time. As you are walking, both the gifts from the past journey and the challenges may show up. You can pause at any time and appreciate the gifts, or pause and consciously let go of old wounds and stories you no longer need.

Pause here, and then periodically add in thoughts to keep the group going or to stimulate new ideas. Leave lots of space between suggestions, watching your group for timing, so you don't overwhelm your participants with suggestions. As you watch your group and listen with your whole body, ideas of what would make the journey more easeful or fruitful will come to you. Here are some examples of thoughts you might add.

You might take a moment on your journey and pause and give back a story, good or bad, that is not yours to live.

You might notice things you have done along the way that were pointing you towards what you are longing for now.

You might notice, where you got stuck or where you were really happy or where you made a new friend who was pivotal or where you really believed in something with all your heart.

You might find some connections to what you want to develop more in your life now, or maybe you will find the roots of your magic that you are manifesting right now.

Just keep walking and reviewing your life and see what comes up to guide you on your path ahead.

When you feel complete, just pause at your ending point until the whole room has come to their ending, taking a moment to land yourself and to enjoy the beauty of seeing others on their journey.

Pause here again until everyone is complete. You may need the participants to complete due to time constraints or because only a couple of people are still going and the rest of your group is complete. You can just ask the group to take the next few minutes to find an ending to this exploration.

Now find a partner and share whatever you wish from that experience—maybe your drawing and what you found along the way, maybe what you are letting go of or what your are reclaiming.

If you have a group that likes to journal, they may want to pause and write some of their insights down before going on to the next task.

The first time I did a version of this, I remembered one of the happiest memories of my childhood, which had been long buried: a play that I had staged and directed in my neighborhood when I was in third grade. I had found an old record, scratched and dusty, that played the story of Hansel and Gretel, with music that played in the background and between the scenes. The sound was a little rough, but it was there. I gathered all the kids in the neighborhood and a couple of live-in grandmothers for rehearsals in Betty's basement. Betty was a neighbor who was always loving and kind to me, and I'm sure she was also aware of the abuse and unhappiness in my family.

We created a little stage in her basement by hanging curtains, made pictures with our crayons of trees and wicked witches to hang around on the walls, created costumes out of old clothes, made dances to go with the music in between scenes, and acted out the whole story as the record played in the background. We had a performance for the neighborhood in the end, though I don't know who actually attended. I was, of course, the director—very bossy I'm sure, and loving too—having a wonderful time dipping into my genius and my vision for the first time.

I share this as an example of how obviously the threads of our health and our life purpose show up when we allow that information to bubble up. It is amazing to me how much that one experience, when I was nine years old, reflects the model we use with communities in Turning the Wheel today.

This memory is not only deeply connected to the work I do today everywhere I go, but also to what makes me happy still. I love to design and stage a show with sets, costumes, music, and a very diverse group of people working together to bring through their magic and their stories.

Task 2: "Journey to Joy"

After a short break and time to get a drink of water, you can guide your group through the next task. If you are doing this on another day, or even after lunch, you will want to warm your group up again.

To prepare for this exercise, look at the "Journey to Joy" worksheet (p. 266 in the "Resources" section). This worksheet was originally made for a quiet writing exercise, so it has a lot of questions on it: different ways of looking at the same issue. For this movement version, you can choose three or four of the questions, so the exercise doesn't take too long. You will know the best ones for your group. When your group looks at their copy of the worksheet you can tell them which questions you will be using. Then participants can explore the other questions on their own if they get intrigued.

Our second task for Baba Yaga, our witch in the forest, is to take a journey into our inner landscape and to gather information for her. You can begin by placing your "Journey to Joy" sheet beside you on the floor. As we go, just let yourself effortlessly answer these questions with whatever comes up as you move and sound in your body, letting you body answer first.

Imagine this piece of paper is your map into the forest and you are carrying a basket on your journey that you will fill up as you go with all the wonderful things that you are finding in the deep forest of your interior.

I will take you through some of the questions by speaking them out loud to you. As we travel together on this journey, just let the interior pathways of your body guide you through the pathways of the forest.

Now just close your eyes and visualize yourself heading into the inside of your body, moving through all the complex pathways and intersections of muscles and vessels and ligaments and bones and joints and organs, easing down into the core of your body and the deep easy "knowing" in your body. Notice where the open spaces are and let your fluids take you into and around these open spaces in your body, relaxing into the flow of your fluids.

Pause here to let participants deepen into their bodies with the music. When you feel your group is ready you can ask the first question you have chosen on the "Journey to Joy" sheet.

When you hear me ask a question, let your body answer, with moving, sounding, and breathing. Let the question just float around in your body and into your consciousness for a few moments. Then turn to your paper and write a few sentences in response, or maybe just some one word cues that will help you remember what floated up out of your body.

When you are ready, close your eyes again and drop gently back into the interior of your body. Relax back into your fluids and feel them carrying you around in your open spaces again. Move and breathe into those spaces and feel the easy weaving of your energies together.

Keep going back and forth with your group between asking questions and returning them to the interior body journey and the fluids. You can vary the language each time you return to the body, based on what you are feeling the group needs by tuning into your intuition, your own "body knowing," What will help them drop back in? How long are they comfortable being there? What metaphors might help them drop more deeply in?

When you have finished asking all the questions you have chosen and letting each person move and write, you can complete this task with some delicious free movement time.

As you emerge from this journey, begin moving gently in the space and see what your body wants to do. Let your body lead and have fun.

Play with others if you wish or move on your own if that feels better to you.

Ask your musician to play some sweet music and to vary the rhythm and mood so that it gathers up all the different moods in the room. When you are ready you can close this task with some sharing.

Take a few minutes to find an ending to your movement for now.

Make your way to a partner. Share your experience with this person and see if anything new comes up for you as you share and listen. This is a great opportunity to practice listening from a "yes" place, and to practice sharing with abandon.

Facilitation Suggestions

As you are guiding folks through this exercise, some participants write a lot and would spend the whole time on one question while others have a one-word answer. When most people in the group have finished, I use cues like:

Take a few more minutes to finish this question for now. You can always come back to these thoughts later.

Or

Take a few moments to finish the thought you are on now and then let your body rest back into movement.

I also quietly encourage those who are complete to read over their writing and add in any new thoughts that come up, or just to take a few moments to rest while others complete.

Variation: This can also be done as a writing exercise with no movement, or as a simple interview exercise, where the participants ask each other the questions and write the answers for each other. Some folks do better if they can talk out loud and not be distracted by writing, while others need to be alone and quiet to feel and write. Also, it might provide a rest for your group if you have been moving a lot.

A vibrant young woman who had been an enthusiastic participant in the workshop came up to me in tears when I first presented this as a simple writing exercise with no movement. She felt completely baffled by the questions and even a little tricked, like she didn't come here to do writing assignments. I had noticed that she was always eager and enlivened during any movement exercise we did, so I suggested that she and I go into the next room and answer the questions out loud while moving and breathing together.

We began to take the questions one at a time, moving around each other and in the room and sharing thoughts about them. Within a few moments she was easily finding answers and insights to the questions, laughing and talking and often surprised by her own thoughts. At the end of playing with each question, she dropped down to her paper on the floor and wrote single word cues to help her remember what she had discovered. I ultimately went back to the group and she continued on by herself, moving and talking out loud to herself as she explored each question.

As I was returning to the room, I was surprised by a very beautiful group mind, group love moment that just popped in spontaneously. Most of the folks in the room had finished the writing and had heard some of what was going on in the next room. They all suddenly decided at the same moment to join her in the next room, bringing their papers along, and started moving and talking out loud and dropping down to write on their papers.

She was ecstatic, blown away by the support and also clearly seeing that the others were all gaining new insights as they went, learning another way to access information from witnessing her process in love and acceptance. She was not only being affirmed, she was leading as well. Her challenges became her gift and gifted others as well. Since that beautiful learning, we usually present this exercise with movement.

As we talked more later, I learned that as a child she had a very difficult time with writing and spelling and had been shamed a lot by her teachers. They had suggested that she just wasn't trying very hard and that she just needed to apply herself. In fact, she is a very kinesthetic learner and integrates and understands new and very complex concepts easily if she is allowed to move as she is thinking.

I am always grateful for the courage of those who step up to tell the truth about their experience and ask for what they want. It is such a gift to us all.

Task 3: "Waking Dreamtime"

Our third task is the most delicious and empowering of all.

Our wise and demanding Baba Yaga now sends us into the land of dreams to reclaim even more pieces of our scattered, sacred psyche. Once you have done this with witnesses you can do it every day as part of your own moving meditation.

I created this journey after doing an informal workshop with a beautiful Australian aboriginal man (truly a Baba Yaga for me) who was traveling the United States and came to stay at my friend Diana's house. He spent time just being with us and teaching about the beliefs and practices he based his life on. I was in a Jungian dream group at the time and was very taken with the idea of waking dreams that he presented.

What I took away from my time with him, some 25 years ago, was that I could dream the life I wanted into existence, for my children and myself exactly as I wanted it to be. Somehow the metaphor of "waking dreaming" really clicked for me and from that day on I proceeded to do that with all my heart and soul, and the direction I took in my life was drastically changed.

We have done this "Waking Dreamtime" exercise with literally hundreds of groups, ranging in age from 16 to 93, and it always substantially deepens the connections in the whole group. Everyone, without exception, discovers new information about themselves and their journey. A teen found the gift in her learning challenges. An elder discovered a new way to view moving into an assisted living facility. A mother reconnected with her love for her children. A husband remembered why he fell in love his wife and envisioned a new direction for his career. A young woman fell in love with her body. And a very wealthy adult discovered a new direction for his energy and his money. Most of all, there have been countless testimonials of dreamers falling more in love with themselves and having the magical experience of touching their own innate and glowing goodness.

Facilitation Suggestions

I begin this exploration with the "Gossamer Threads" dance, described below, so the group is connected before taking such a deep journey. It helps create safety for the participants, as each person drops into a more loving and open place.

As you will see below, I set up the groups and all the directions for the "Dreamtime" and the instructions for the waking dream experience first, and then back up and bring them into their groups right out of the "Gossamer Threads" dance without pausing.

Let's begin by making circles of five (or four if your group is smaller), and take a moment to connect and to be sure you know everyone's name. I am going to tell you what we are going to do in this circle and then we will back up and do a very special exercise that will prepare us for this dream and guide us back into this group.

Each one of you is going to have a chance to go into the middle of this beautiful circle of witnesses and let your body and your soul dream your life ahead. Remember your body and soul contain each other, so one leads back to the other in a moving spiral of evolution.

You will get to spend five minutes dropping into your body and your authentic movement, moment by moment, just allowing your dream to emerge. As the mover, you can use this time any way you wish, moving a lot or a little, quickly or slowly, standing or sitting or laying down, making sound or remaining silent, etc.

The circle around you is like a womb of love and protection, witnessing you with unconditional acceptance and supporting the birth of your dream. I will ring a bell when your time is up, and you will then take your time to come out of your dream and back into the circle to become a midwife for the next person. As one person slowly leaves the circle, another gently enters so the circle in never completely empty.

As a witness and keeper of the womb you can move and gently sound and experiment with how to truly unconditionally reflect the dreamer over and over, paying attention to your breath and to releasing any stories you may be making up about the dreamer or about yourself. The gift you are giving the dreamer is to be unconditionally present in the dream state with them. The dreamer is gifting you with the incredible honor of witnessing their authentic journey to self.

Take a moment in your group and decide now who will go first when we get to this part of the exercise. Also, take a look at who is here with you, as we will come back in a few minutes to this group—so maybe hold hands a minute and see who is there.

"Gossamer Threads"

OK, let's begin with this exercise of connection. Spread out into the room and find a place to stand that feels like your own. As you stand there just drop into your feet, let your breath be easy, and feel the little small movements internally that move you back and forth and that keep your body upright. Allow those movements to be there in your stillness.

Feel the energy from the center of the earth coming up from below to support you and hold you and the power of gravity coming down from the heavens and surrounding you on all sides. Let yourself relax into that support and rest into this moment in your body.

Now tune into the bodies around you, on your sides and behind you and in front of you, feeling the different energies in the room. As you are ready, begin to build a web of connection to everyone in the room. Just send, in your mind's eye, a beautiful silken gossamer thread from your hand to the top of somebody's head, from your foot to an elbow, from your heart to a belly, from your back to a lung, from your toes to somebody's fingers, visualizing and feeling the web of connection growing.

Pause here and leave time for the room to get connected before moving on to the next step.

When you are ready, you can begin to actually gesture with your arms and your whole body as you send a thread across the room into somebody's torso and see it land, then send another one out, maybe this one close to the floor, or flying in an arc across the ceiling. Let yourself begin to move through the room sending these silken threads of connection out everywhere and feeling your body receiving them from others, feeling the pull and flow of the web of connections, creating your own gossamer threads dance. You might wrap a whole web of love around one person or shower strings of webs down another person's whole body. You might pause and wrap yourself in some loving threads and feel all the beautiful connections of love coming your way.

Now pause, again, allowing the gossamer threads dance to develop fully and the joy and fun in the room to build. Then, using the cue below, move the group into the dream circles that they formed at the beginning of this task.

"Waking Dreamtime"
Now allow these threads to pull and guide you gently and silently into your dream circle group. As you gather together, move and breathe together and let all those threads of connection ground you into a safe and loving circle of witnesses.

Remember who was going first and as the first person enters into the circle, the witnesses will shift all of their focus and energy towards the dreamer, moving and breathing with them, supporting and loving their courage and their dream. Mover, just let your body find its own way, following your deep body wisdom into dreamtime.

When you hear the bell you will know to take a few moments to come back to the room, open your eyes and return to the circle. Then, as you return to the circle, a new person will gently enter the circle.

Facilitation Suggestions

At the end of this exercise the groups naturally want to come closer in their circle and stay together for a few minutes. You can suggest to each circle quietly and individually as they complete that they tone and sound and breathe together to close.

If one group finishes a little before another just have them close their circle in a little and tone and sound together as they wait.

The music for this exercise is very important. Ask your musician to play something that helps to create a quiet mood, one that will help to create a safe and sacred space.

This dreaming experience is a deep dive for any group, and it is important for the facilitator to stay present throughout, holding and witnessing the room in love. It is also good to leave some time for the dream groups to talk and share their experiences with each other before moving on.

After a break, you can lead your group into the next step of this exercise, preparing to walk the path forward, empowered to show up and create the life they want. Often this next step happens the next day or the next time we meet if we are doing a weekly gathering. It depends on how deeply your group goes into the previous three tasks.

Walking the Path Forward

I reach for my inner knowing to guide me forward as I open new pathways of energetically loving myself.

And so we have completed the three tasks for Baba Yaga. We have walked and drawn our past story, enjoying the good memories and releasing the ones we no longer need. We have gone on a journey to find what gives us joy, what it is we really want, and we have integrated all of that into our bodies as we let our bodies dream the story that we want to create. We are now ready to take all of these pieces we have gathered, all that we have remembered about our joy, and all that we have dreamed in our bodies, and take the next step into our empowered, embodied, manifesting lives.

Once again we begin with tuning into the miraculous pathways that run all through our inner landscape. The most effective transition into creating new pathways forward is to weave the internal web inside your body first, finding the internal connections and opening them all up to flowing and working together. Then you can build the web outside of your body on the strength and flexibility of that internal web.

Pathways in the Brain

The first place we go for pathways is the brain, which is in communication with all the messengers in our body. The brain makes connections, creates new synapses, and builds new neurological patterns based on our experiences. Every thought you have produces a chemical that tells you how to feel. Then you feel that, which produces another thought and so on. Our brain simply does what we tell it to do and believes what we tell it to believe. Our joy or our suffering is very simply linked to what we are telling ourselves.

We also know that the back of the spine, where our incoming body sensations are processed by our peptides, is one of the particularly busy and amazing pathmakers inside us. These neuropeptides are the messenger molecules in our bodies that actually run around and talk to our cells. They connect us to all points in our bodies by weaving the body's organs and systems into a single web that reacts to our internal and our external environment. Peptides are the receptors on the cells for the brain that speak to the brain, like the eyes and ears for the cells.

So, as we set out to create a new path that is uniquely our own, we are interested in telling our brains to send new and positive messages to these peptides, which they can then carry to our cells and turn on the flow of these cellular fluids as they respond with joy to these new stories we are telling.

The journey ahead is an empowering and transformative pathway to turning on those feel-good stories in our bodies.

We will dive into your amazing fluid system, and discover the connection of our bodies with the ancient healing power of the waters of the earth.

And from there we will create a loving and intimate encounter with your higher self, your deep inner knowing, and your inner child. Connecting with your higher self or your "wise guardian" inside is a powerful tool to have as you commit to discovering more of you own unique path through life. And the power of your own creative and enthusiastic inner child is beyond calculation.

We will begin with getting tuned into our body sensations and then move into total immersion in the waters of the womb. You can do this with a group or on your own, using the audio recording online (www.turningthewheel.org/audio).

Let's begin walking in the space, feeling your feet on the floor, noticing your breath moving easefully through your body, listening to the rhythms of your body, the pulsing of your fluids. Relax your belly…, your jaw…, your fingers…, the back of your neck…, the space behind your eyes.…

Scan your body for a place that feels good, focus on that place, give it attention, let it move and, see if it has any sound to express. Find another place that feels good. Let the two of them dance together, expand together. Find another place that feels good and invite that place into the dance, and then another. Notice the good feelings spreading and growing as you keep giving attention to what feels good.

Have fun playing and dancing with all these parts that feel good and want to come out and play. Interact with others in the group if you wish and let your happy energy play with their good energy.

Keep moving and let go of all instructions and listen to your body. What does your body want right now? What wants to happen in this moment… and in this moment… and in this moment? For the next 10 minutes, just explore your own energy and impulses from one moment to the next. Sound is fine, too. Your body loves the sound of your voice. You may be moving very slowly or very quickly—this is your own "seeking-self" dance. What is authentically emerging from you right now?

Taking your time, use the next few minutes to complete this exploration and slowly find a comfortable spot on the floor and drop down into a relaxed position in your body, letting your breath be easy and natural. You may want to lay on your side or on your back with your legs bent or just flat on the floor. Take the time you need to transition.

"Waters of the Womb"

Take a nice deep belly breath and let yourself come into the interior of your body and feel your fluids effortlessly moving in and out of your cells, releasing any tight sensations in your body to the breath.

Visualize space opening up in your body so all the fluids can flow freely through and around your bones and your muscles, and bathe your body in their healing energy. Notice any place that is contracted or tight and let it float open to receive the soothing flow of the fluids.

Now slowly begin to imagine that your body is floating freely in the waters of the womb of the great mother. Feel your whole body release into these warm and welcoming fluids, supporting you as you relax into their gentle care.

Just let your body drift from side to side, folding up and extending out in those waters, slowly opening and closing, expanding and contracting, easy and free in the warm waters. Maybe an arm floats slowly up, like in a slow motion dream, or your head is slowly turning, floating free.

These waters are pure and free of any confusion or ambivalence or stress. Your limbs are free and floating, you are light and totally supported by these warm waters. You don't even have to worry about breathing.

You are totally held in these waters, swimming in the constant and loving stream of well-being that is always there for you, rocking you, cradling you.

I leave space here for the group to explore this before going on, occasionally adding little releasing cues, based on what I see happening in the room like:

Feel the water flowing gently around you and moving your arms and legs as they float free.

Let your whole body release to the warm waters and the gentle rocking motion of this watery womb.

Notice if you are contracted anywhere and gently release that into the fluids.

When your group has had plenty of time to find this fluid state of being in their bodies, add in these thoughts.

Feel your fluids connecting with all the waters of the earth and all the paths those fluids have traveled, all the canyons they have carved, and all the life they have sustained, including your own amazing body. They are wise and old and always singing you lullabies of love and comfort.

Sing back to them. Sing them a sweet little love song of gratitude.

Sing a love song to your body from the waters of the earth, allowing that love to infuse the fluids moving through all the layers of your body. Let the fluids of your body release you into a floating peaceful energy, feel your skin dissolving away as you merge with the waters, resonating with the vibrations of the waters of the earth.

You will want to let your group spend time here in these watery vibrations, held by beautiful music and the loving energy you are surrounding them with. When you see and feel that the group is ready to move on, you can slowly transition them back into the room and ultimately up to standing.

As you are ready, slowly begin to emerge from these waters into the room of beautiful beings around you, maybe slowly crawling out on to the land, or floating up into a sitting position and then back down and then back up, taking your time to come back, noticing how your body is feeling.

As you come more and more into the room, remember the ease and the love you felt in those waters and let that energy come with you.

Keep moving and flowing up out of the water, taking your time to blink your eyes open and see the room and the light in the room, the people around you.

When you are ready, Let yourself easefully float up into the space until you are standing, still moving in your liquid system, still flowing and "fluidy," bringing all of that well-being into your waking life.

As you are ready, begin moving through the room—passing by others, but staying tuned to yourself for now, and letting your fluids lead.

Here the facilitator pauses again, giving everyone in the group time to arrive at this point in their own flow. More gentle cues may be needed along the way to get everybody up and moving. Once they are all up and moving in their fluids through the room, you can guide them through the final step.

"The Wise Guardian and the Child"

As you are moving through the room look off into the distant horizon and see an ocean. Start walking over the dunes towards the ocean, smelling and feeling the change in the air, the salty moisture. As you get closer notice the sound of the waves getting louder and the breeze picking up.

Maybe you hear the seagulls, or see them circling around. Let the feelings that you have when you are near the ocean come up and pause as you come over the hill and actually see the ocean and the waves and the birds.

Keep walking up to the edge of the water and you will see a luminous spirit being emerging out of the water and coming towards you, reaching out to you. Reach out and take hands with this wise guardian, who is always with you and is a part of your beautiful self, your higher self. Look into the eyes of this spirit being, who is loving you and so glad to see you, and who is appreciating all that is you.

This wise inner guide is glad you that you are coming from your journey in the waters to connect and appreciate this very important part of yourself, a part that you can always depend on, and who is always there for you. Look into the eyes of this being and let yourself bathe in the unconditional love, the sweet kindness, and the tender wisdom that is pouring down over your body from this luminous being.

Now take a moment and change places with your wise guardian. Step into the energy of your wise guardian and become him or her for a moment. Look over at yourself through the eyes of this being— seeing all the love you bring to others and all of your kindness and wisdom shining out, seeing how absolutely whole and authentic you are in this very moment, seeing all that is breathtaking about you.

Now come back into your body and as you look out again at your spirit guide, notice that he or she has a gift for you, a little piece of wisdom for you to take forward with you on your new journey. Open up your heart and your hands and receive this gift, expressing your gratitude in any way you wish.

Take a moment to be with this gift and truly let it in.

Before you head back over the dunes, look back over your shoulder and you will see your little child running towards you. She or he wants to play and dance with you and your wise ocean being. Scoop this little one up and the three of you run and dance and play together there on the edge of the water.

See who else is there playing by the ocean and dance together if you wish, letting all the beautiful trios of beings play together. Maybe you will share the gift you received, or dance with it, or just feel the impact of this gift in your body as you dance.

Let your "Wise Guardian" return to the waters, and your child snuggle back inside you as you complete this dance, finding your way back into the circle in the room.

Facilitation Suggestions

Building up to fun and joyful music is very important here.

Gather your group up in a circle as they are winding down and close by grounding together as a group with a "Sounding Circle" (p. 281 in the "Resources" section) that you can guide with soft directions towards a prayer of gratitude, suggesting quietly to the participants that they might make sounds of gratitude and praise or hum a little of song of gratitude to their spirit guide or their higher self.

As the sounding comes to silence let everyone stand in that silence for a few moments and then have them take a deep breath and blink their eyes open and come back in the room, connecting to each other with their eyes.

When they are ready, you can guide them to find a partner and take a few moments to go to a quiet, still place with this partner, connecting from their breath and their heart.

Then they can share about this experience with their partner.

Close with giving them time to write in their journal.

Celebration, Acting As If

I step into the moving and changing mystery of each day, walking a path of celebration and joyful evolution.

You have now completed a long and very rich journey of self-exploration, including completing the three tasks for Baba Yaga and making friends with your higher self. So you are ready to walk the path forward creating the future you want for yourself. As we step onto this path, we will "Act As If" we already have everything we want, which of course we do. It is all just waiting there for you to allow it in. We know that our beliefs structure our reality, and so it is exciting that we can truly choose to manifest a life that is in alignment with our dreams and our gifts and our joy.

When I was in the second grade, I was in a Bluebird group (the first step before becoming a Camp Fire Girl) with two leaders who were very kind and patient and who were the beginning of my awareness that what was happening in my family was not the norm. Coming from my abusive home, I was already very defended, argued a lot, and often felt frightened, which I covered with bravado and stubbornness. I was certainly not an easy child to integrate into the group,

217

and they were both consistently incredibly kind and loving to me. My inner path toward healing began with these two beautiful women.

One of the women, Barbara Sternberg, a wise and powerful woman and dear friend and guide, (who lived to be 93), gave me a game to play when I was at home, called "Act as If." It was an extremely creative lifeline that she gave me to survive my home environment. From that day on, my virtual life, my "Act as If," became my dream of how it could be. The harshness of the verbal and physical violence did not change, but now I had a conscious vision.

When I was nine years old and ironing most of every Saturday, I lived through those hours of ironing making up my life—wonderful imaginary birthday parties with presents wrapped with beautiful bows, time with my mother making cookies and laughing, playing safely with dolls and singing songs in the orchard, dance classes where I had those little pink ballet shoes I so longed for, and I was always the star of the performance twirling ecstatically around in my mind's eye, all in my imagination.

It was such profound genius on Barbara's part, as I began to create in my mind the world I wanted to live in and the kinds of people I wanted there and what we would do together. I am living that vision now and I have every one of those people that I imagined would be there.

I began to celebrate what I wanted to have happen "as if" it had already happened. I was sending out pure heartfelt desire to the universe, clear, and detailed, and in the midst of ongoing unconscionable abuse, some part of me thrived.

Every year a new beautiful person—a neighbor, a teacher, a doctor, a friend's mother—reached out to me and guided me out of my family story into more and more possibility. It was a long journey out, and it created in me the wisdom and compassion and knowing that is the basis for all my work with Turning the Wheel today.

I realize there might have been the danger that I would mix up reality with my imaginary musings, but instead I learned about the power of positive attraction very young!

Today I have the an incredibly blessed life with my seven amazing and loving children and their wonderful partners, with my eight outrageously beautiful grandchildren, with my indescribably generous and deeply committed Turning the Wheel family, with friends who love and nurture me, with work that I love and that makes a difference on the earth, and with a strong, healthy, and joyful body that carries me forward into the mysteries of the unknown every day. The idea that you do not have to change the past to create a new future echoes in my life over and over again, and in the lives of those I am privileged to play with every day.

"Five Years Forward"

So we have arrived at the completion ritual for the "Reclaiming Our Path" journey. Creating a virtual reality, "acting as if," is a powerful visualization tool, so take your time and enjoy this journey into your future life, remembering that past, present, and future are all really one in the quantum world.

This is really fun to do in a group. It ramps up the positive energy, and can create a whole community of people committed to evolving in joy, vibrationally supporting each other on their positive creative paths.

Begin walking in the room and let yourself visualize a place in nature where you feel strong and peaceful at the same time. This could be a place you have been, or a place you want to go. It could be the top of a mountain or in a beautiful mountain meadow. Maybe you are standing at the edge of the ocean or in the blowing wind on the cliffs above the ocean, or looking out over a desert landscape as the sun is setting.

Walk around in this place and feel how good it feels to be there. Notice the smells and the light and the sounds, the feeling in the air. Let yourself fully arrive in this place you have chosen.

This place of empowerment and peace will be your starting point for your path forward. Step on to this path, walking forward, letting your feet just choose the way. As you are walking feel your energy moving forward in time into what you want for your life, into the freedom and joy that you are creating now for your life ahead.

Let your movement on the path reflect those feelings, maybe dancing, laughing, skipping, sounding, or whatever is coming up from your body. As you move forward into your future, you are gathering bits and pieces along the way to put in your basket of resources. What new gifts are emerging as you walk this forward path?

Pause when you feel an impulse to and notice these gifts that are already in place for you. Pick them up, put them in your basket, and take them with you as you go.

The guardians of old stories, fixed habits and attitudes, may also crop up for you along the path. Try using humor and play to loosen their grip. Love them, thank them for the value they once provided, and invite them to play and dance with you, transforming them into allies.

Try listening with your whole body to the messages along your path. Maybe you will find bits of your story in the stones along the path. There might be running water in the distance whispering guidance to you, or the trees might answer you in a soft wind.

Now let yourself imagine that this piece of your journey is finding a place to pause and that you have arrived at five years ahead and picture your life just the way you want it to be.

The facilitator would slowly ask these questions, watching the responses of the bodies in the group for timing. You might have a different question come up as you tune into your group, or maybe you will only ask some of these questions. Take your time, creating space for your group to take their time.

What are you doing?
Who is there with you?
Where are you living?
Who is in your basket that will support you?
How are you spending your time?

How do you feel about yourself?

What gifts have you manifested into the world?

What do you hear if you listen very carefully?

Let the whole virtual reality manifest for you in your whole body, with all of your cells and fluids joining in the story.

Now move and breathe and let yourself embrace this new story, feeling your fluids moving this reality into all of your cells and flowing it through your blood stream, your life's blood.

How does your body want to move this new story, breathe this new story, sound this new story?

How do you walk through the room as you embrace this reality?

Scan your whole body, just noticing how it feels, from your toes to the top of your head.

As you begin to see others in the room, notice how you want to relate to them, and if they look different to you as well. Maybe you will reach out and have a moment of moving and playing with them, or just connecting for a moment, appreciating your conscious friends who are traveling on this journey with you.

Slowly bring this exploration to a close for now, pausing to breathe and feel your feet on the floor, letting all that you have done settle down into the core of your body.

When you feel ready to check in, make your way to a partner and take turns telling your stories to each other "as if" they have already happened. You may want to take a few moments after sharing to write in your journal.

Facilitation Suggestions

This journey involves a lot of sounding and movement and particularly needs powerful, non-rhythmical, transformative music that has no words and helps create a safe container. We did this journey at our summer retreat with incredibly sacred and inspiring music that Jesse Manno played for us. (His music is available at his website, *spot.colorado. edu/~manno).*

If you don't have a musician to play with you, there are also some suggestions of recorded music you could use on p. 331 in the "Resources" section. Many of you will have something in your music collection that you know would be just perfect.

You could also have your group complete this exercise by drawing the path they just took and decorating it with words and feathers and jewels, or rocks and shells and leaves, to honor their new journey.

The "May I, May You" exercise (p. 188) is a great completion for this exploration. Or in place of the unstructured sharing at the end, each person could share their story "as if" it has already happened. The listener could then move their response to that sharing.

More "Act As If" Activities to Celebrate

Here are some less involved, simple, and fun ways to celebrate "as if" your wishes and dreams were already in place, or "as if" what you are wanting in your life has already happened. You can also use these activities as fun ways to increase your positive vibration.

"A Joyful Dance"

Put on some happy music to help create a fun environment. Begin moving around the room, dancing and expressing with sound or song the way you will feel when a dream you have is realized.

How do you hold your shoulders? Is your heart throbbing and speaking to you? What are your feet doing, your fingers, your eyes? Notice the energy that is flowing through your body.

Keep playing and moving until your whole body is tingling and happy, and see your dream as a reality in this very moment.

"A Celebration Collage"

Create a celebration collage to hang on the wall, or to put in your kitchen window to remind you that all you want is already here, waiting for you to embrace it.

You can go to a local craft or sewing store and get little sparkling jewels, ribbons, feathers, and sequins to glue on your paper. Use bits of beautiful paper you have saved from presents, or other odd bits you have kept, like single earrings, buttons, or shells.

Add joyful words you cut out of magazines and/or images you love. You will be surprised how much fun you have and how valuable this reminder will be for you.

There is no right or wrong way to do this. Just let your little child out to play and have a blast gluing and cutting and sticking things on!

This is fun to do with a group of friends as well. You could combine this activity with the party below.

"Brainstorm Party"

Invite your friends over for a party to celebrate with you and brainstorm positive paths ahead on big pieces of paper you have posted on the wall. There could be a space for them to write all the ways they would like to help, and another space for all the things they are grateful for about you and appreciate about you, and another space for possible resources they know about that would help you realize your dream.

Provide lots of healthy food and drinks to share with your tribe as a gesture of gratitude to them, and as a signal to your brain that you are celebrating.

You could also have each of them think of a dream of their own and all visualize together and create the celebration collages in the exercise above together.

At the end of the gathering, you might write in your journal all of the positive words of appreciation and recognition that you heard others saying to you about your life and your accomplishments.

Make this celebration yours. Use whatever resonates for you to create your virtual reality. It might be the smell of the cake you will bake to celebrate, or seeing in your mind's eye the letter of praise your friend will send you, or simply gathering folks around you who love and support you so your energy goes even more towards "yes."

Conclusion

And so, as we complete the journey around the healing mandala, we end up back where we started this book, remembering that the real change point is in being willing to say "yes" to ourselves on a consistent and reliable basis. What do I want, what makes me smile, what brings ease to my body?

And that, in turn, takes us to falling even more passionately and enthusiastically in love with ourselves. From that place of deep self-love, you are automatically a healing force for every person who comes into your life and for the whole earth as your loving energy becomes a part of the collective unconscious that informs and moves us all.

All of life is really about getting present and then more present in our bodies, following all of our inner guides into living a life of "What wants to happen, right now, in this moment?" Every one of those moments is an incredible opportunity for your life to manifest in joyful service to this planet and to the folks who perch so precariously on it.

My prayer is that as you complete this book, you have moved and sounded and played and laughed right into the center of your authentic self, into the center of the "The Body Now" mandala. I happily imagine that you are out in your communities expressing your unique essence gifts in unbridled joy, bringing that joy to others and to the children of this earth.

Resources

Appreciations

Appreciations are the basic building blocks for a good life on every level all the time. Just increasing the number of appreciations we think and speak to ourselves, and to each other, each day is the only spiritual practice we would ever need to become a fully evolved human being. Here are some questions you could ask yourself to stimulate appreciations and some sentence stems you could use to get started on expressing appreciations.

For Self

What am I grateful for about the earth, the sky, the animals, the waters, the winds, the trees…?

What do I appreciate about my body, my brain, my health, my energy, my essence…?

What do I appreciate about my home, my family and children, my partner, my friends, my work, my dreams…?

What do I appreciate about my skills, my gifts, my knowledge…?

What do I appreciate about my creativity, the way I dress, the way I create my living space…?

For Others
What could you appreciate about this person right in this moment?

What is particularly wonderful, amazing, or awesome about this person?

What is unique about this person's contribution to the world?

How does this person show up in my life, in community, in groups?

What strengths do I notice about this person?

How does this person help me or others?

What is unusual or interesting about how this person uses their creativity?

How has this person said yes to me?

What makes me happy when I am around this person?

How does this person give me attention?

What are ways this person always shows up?

What agreements does this person always keep?

What amazing things has this person already done in their life?

What have I learned from this person?

How has this person supported me in my journey?

How does this person manage change or challenges?

How does this person relate to spirit?

Some Appreciation Sentence Stems
I love the way I/you…

I love how I/you…

I notice I/you…

Thank you for…

I am grateful that…

I see my/your…

I appreciate that I/you have…

I appreciate my/your…

I am amazed at…

I consistently see…

Look for new ways of appreciation—Shine a light!

Art Projects

We have created many different projects for participants to create sacred art that will affirm and reinforce their insights and body knowing when they return home. The projects can serve as a reminder to move and play each day or to meditate or sing. They can remind us to love ourselves, to keep a commitment we have made, or to simply feel good about our creative expression.

Recently we finished a totem project in a women's group I was leading. One woman had never done an art project. She made an incredibly stunning and expressive totem, and I watched her admire her work for the rest of the class. She could not get over the fact that she had actually created this beautiful little sculptural object.

As well as providing a rest in a long day of moving, art projects bring in another way to express our creative beings, and for some, they offer an easier avenue than moving in our bodies. I always tie these into the theme of the day, like putting our actions steps inside treasure boxes or creating postcards of self-love to mail home to ourselves.

These projects have been tested with many different populations, ages, and abilities, and they are set up for success. The materials you provide have a lot to do with that. We are always careful to choose colors that all are beautiful together, materials that are easy to use, and directions that are simple and accessible.

We also create a few of each project ahead as samples of what the product can look like at the end, making sure the samples are very different from each other. We have found this to be very helpful in inspiring each group. It is important to encourage your participants to create their own version, doing whatever is calling to them in the moment.

We always work without talking during the art projects with beautiful music playing, so the choices people are making come from a place of quiet reflection or uninterrupted flow. It is good to start with some moving and breathing to get everyone in their bodies and release tension. Then folks can quietly come to their working place on the floor or at a table and begin.

No matter what people have created with these projects, their result is always amazing, and this has been true for 30 years with thousands of people.

In the following pages you will a find broad range of ideas, from quick and easy projects that could be completed in an hour or so to weeklong projects. It is a good idea to try these yourself first before bringing them to your group.

Decoupage Tissue Treasure Boxes

Materials
Little wooden boxes
These come in many different shapes and are very affordable at places like JoAnn's or Michael's.
Tissue paper in many different colors and patterns
I save all the scraps of tissue paper I use for wrapping presents and also watch for good ones when I am out shopping for other things. This works best if the paper is thin. You can also buy packages of all different colors of plain tissue paper.
Mod Podge
This is a decoupage glue available at Michael's or JoAnn's.
Cheap paintbrushes
These are to apply the Mod Podge and they will probably have to be thrown away after a few uses, so get the cheap ones in packages of twelve or more sold at craft stores.
Small plastic cups or bowls or little paper cups
This is to put the Mod Podge in so each person can have their own or two people can share one.
Scissors
You just need a few pairs for those who don't want to tear the tissue.

Directions
Prepare your cups of Mod Podge and set them around the table or on the floor, which has been covered with a plastic cloth for protection. Mod Podge is very hard to get out of anything once it dries. We often work on the floor as we are

in movement spaces with no tables or chairs. You can put a paintbrush by each cup.

Spread all the tissue out in the middle of the room so lots of participants can reach into the pile at one time. You can cut the big pieces of tissue up into smaller pieces so it is easy to choose a lot of different small pieces of different colors.

Each person begins by choosing the box that calls to them, maybe a heart shape, a round shape, a rectangle with a clear top etc. I always make sure to have more than one of each shape so everybody gets the one they want. Often these simple art projects bring out our little kid and we want all the little kids to be happy!

Then each person can choose small pieces of all different patterns and colors of tissue paper. We always tell them not to worry, that they can come back for more or different colors once they get going.

To create a beautiful little jewel of a box, just start tearing the tissue into small pieces and cover each piece with a little Mod Podge to glue it in place on the box. This is a little odd for some folks, as when you decoupage, you glue it on by painting over the top, not underneath it. We always have scissors on hand so that people who want to cut the tissue paper instead of tear it can do that.

Then you just keep layering the tissue on the box overlapping each piece, and even on top of other pieces, folding it around corners and watching it turn into something amazing. This is a simple project that everybody can be successful with and only requires a few materials.

The inside of the box can be covered as well, as long as you watch out for gluing the lid shut.

These creations then need to be set on plastic to dry for several hours, or overnight, depending on the amount of decoupage glue that was applied.

Treasures
Once the boxes are dry you can use them to complete your workshop by having people write their action steps on little pieces of paper and put them in the box. They could write self-love statements and put them in the box to read later.

Each individual could decide how they want to represent what they treasure in themselves or their lives, or what they wish to treasure more.

If you are in nature with your group, people may want to collect little treasures to put in their boxes that symbolize something they want to bring into their lives or something they treasure about themselves.

The wonderful thing about this step is that you can make up anything that fits with your theme or the focus of your workshop. The most important thing is to take time to share with each other and to admire each person's box and treasures.

Other Box Variations

The same basic ideas can be applied to decorating boxes of any kind—little tin mint boxes, round tea cans, and all different shapes and sizes of boxes which you or your participants may have saved—with a great variety of materials. You can use any of the materials listed below in the "Wands" project, for example, instead of tissue, and create spirit boxes, talismans, or wish boxes.

You can use hot glue guns to attach bigger items to the boxes or special tacky glue. You can wrap the boxes in string and tie objects to them or even create a hook and hang them on the wall. Just have fun going from a base idea and making up projects that fit the theme, the skill level, and the timing of your group.

Wands

Materials

Sticks, branches (trimmed or not), chopsticks, etc.

Materials for wrapping and hanging down from the wands:

Ribbons of all colors and widths

Embroidery thread in lots of colors

Yarns with different textures and colors

Sparkling, delicate, gossamer-like thread

Thin wire of many different colors to decorate with or to use to attach beads, stones, or crystals

Beads of all kinds

Rocks and crystals

Seashells

Feathers in many different sizes and colors

Anything jewel-like

Directions

This is a very versatile project that yields surprisingly outrageous results. It can be done with everything from recycled chopsticks to very complex tree branches. Making the wands can take an hour or a whole week, where participants add some things on every day.

Providing lots of variety in materials is one key to success with Wands. Our facilitators often add in beads or stones, rocks, or glass chunks that they are ready to pass on. Old pieces of jewelry can be really great for this too.

There is no gluing with this project, only wrapping and wiring and tying. Be sure to have some samples so participants get the idea of how to use the materials before they begin.

The idea of the wands is that participants will choose colors and objects that have meaning to them, whether intuitively or consciously. For example, we begin our workshops on our healing mandala with awareness, and so the first day we work on the wands we are focusing on awareness and all that we have explored around that, and maybe some of what we have discovered. For some it might be finding colors their inner child loves, or looking for what would represent flowing more in their lives, or a rock to represent a need for grounding. By the time we get to the fourth day when we are focusing on action steps, very different objects are added to the wands.

If you are doing a one-hour project in the middle of a daylong workshop, you would provide a smaller base, like a chopstick, and you might have the participants think about something they want to say "yes" to in their lives, something they would like to remember when they go home, or something new they learned about themselves. It helps to give them a direction to start and then they will take it wherever it needs to go.

Once you have given the directions and established a theme, you can do some guided moving and breathing and releasing into their body wisdom for few minutes, and then let folks begin to decorate their wand without talking. Playing beautiful music will help hold the mood.

It is always good to share at the end in whatever format you like, whether in twos or threes or with the whole group. Sharing helps to ground what is happening and helps your group deepen into connection with each other.

The summer retreat participants who made wands during the week swear they really did work magic in their lives. "Every time I look at the wand I remember the healing cycle and how easy it is to stay feeling good about myself and others. Truly magic for me."

Postcards

Materials
Card stock in beautiful light colors, pre-cut into 5 x 7 inch pieces.
Glue sticks and/or Aleene's Tacky Glue
Self-stick sparkling gems
Feathers
Pompoms
Pipe cleaners in different colors
Sequins, including stars and spirals
Ribbon
Tissue paper
Patterned handmade papers
Magic markers and/or sparkle pens
Envelopes big enough to hold a decorated card with some three-dimensional elements

Directions
These postcards are easy to make and fun for everyone. They can be completed in one hour and make a great break around two in the afternoon during an all-day workshop. They are great for people to take home and put in their kitchen window or on their mirror to help them remember their new story. Variations on this project can work well in many different settings and with many different themes. Some ideas for themes that we have used are described below, but any theme that fits the direction you are heading will help to ground a new beginning.

Themes

Postcard Home

In the "Postcard Home," participants write something they love about themselves, or an affirmation of something they want to bring into their lives, on the back of the card. Then they decorate the front, and when they are done, they put it in a provided envelope and write their address on the envelope. Then you gather all the cards and mail them a couple of weeks after the workshop. It is fun to get a little love note to yourself in the mail, and it helps extend the value of the workshop.

Making a Promise

Another way we use the postcards is to have participants write a sacred promise to themselves on the card. The idea is that this is like a covenant, an unbreakable agreement with yourself. It can be something they are committing to doing for themselves, something that allows them to love themselves or appreciate themselves more or that helps them take care of themselves in some new way.

They could write this promise with colored pens, or glue on word pool words to represent the promise in a short poem. The promise might be written around the edges of the card like a border, or upside down or tiny or huge or crossing over from the front to the back, using both sides any way they want.

Once they have written their words they can honor their agreement by decorating the card with more drawing and coloring, beautiful cut paper symbols, tissue paper flowers, or gluing on wonderful gems. The promise postcards can become very three-dimensional or stay simple and flat. Each one will be as individual as the person who is making it, and they are always amazing.

Remember to leave time for sharing at the end. I always have people move and celebrate this promise in their body, adding sound if they have gotten comfortable with making sounds and song together.

Self-love

Another variation on the postcard exercise would be to write something you want to love more about yourself on the card and then decorate and celebrate that. This is good for all of us and particularly good for folks who are in recovery of some kind.

Trees

Materials

Large pieces of heavy, white butcher paper precut to 2 x 3 feet

Magic markers (including fine-point markers) and/or sparkle pens

Glue sticks and/or Aleene's Tacky Glue

Self-stick sparkling gems

Feathers in many different sizes and colors

Pompoms

Pipe cleaners in different colors

Sequins, including stars and spirals

Tissue paper

Patterned handmade papers

Ribbons of all colors and widths

Embroidery thread in lots of colors

Yarns with different textures and colors

Sparkling, delicate, gossamer-like thread

Thin wire of many different colors to decorate with or to use to attach beads, stones, or crystals

Beads of all kinds

Rocks and crystals

Seashells

Anything jewel-like

Directions

Trees are one of the oldest symbols in the world, showing up in all different cultures and religions and worshipped by many. Trees are very rich in possibilities for symbolic sacred art projects. They give us life here on earth -- one tree provides oxygen for four people for a full day. They protect us from the sun and clean the air, and provide housing for many birds and animals. And they connect us to both the earth and the heavens, with their roots reaching down into the earth and their branches reaching up into the sky.

We have done many different projects with trees over the years, including starting our summer retreat by going to the trees and giving them all the old stories we would like to release as we begin a week of rediscovering more pieces of our authentic selves. We have even gone to the forest in the northwest (guided by Vickie Dodd) to listen to the ancient tress and seek their wisdom.

In our most recent summer retreat we used trees as our sacred art project for representing our movement around the healing mandala throughout the week. The 40 pieces of truly astounding art that were showcased on the walls at the end of week were breathtaking, and each one was radically different from the other.

Have each of your participants begin by drawing a simple outline of a tree on their paper any way they want. They can turn the paper either direction and have a taller tree or a wider tree.

The amazing thing about trees is they can represent the past, present, and future all at once, with the roots being the past, the trunk holding the present, and the branches reaching into the future.

You can also look at the roots as what grounds us and keeps us steady, the trunk as our core knowing and strength, and the branches as our wishes and hopes and dreams.

You can see how you can sculpt the symbolism to match the work you are doing with your group. For example, maybe your group wants to focus on what gifts they already have in their core being (trunk), and how to ground those gifts in practical skills (roots), and then put actions steps in the branches to manifest those gifts.

We often have our groups start with the roots, where they can look at everything from their ancestors' support, to past stories they are ready to release into the earth, to gifts that have been hidden from them that they are ready to have emerge. What gifts do they bring forward from their history or what gifts are there for them to manifest?

You can spin this any way that will serve your group and follow their lead into a wonderful symbolic exploration into their inner landscape. Just give them a frame to begin and let them use the materials you have provided to explore and create their own amazing story in their tree.

Mandala

Materials

Sheets of colored poster board for the base, cut into 14 x 14 inch squares.

This is available at any art store in different weights. I get lots of different colors so each person can choose the color they want. It doesn't have to be too heavy, just stiff enough to provide a good base. You can take the paper to somewhere like Fed Ex/Kinko's and cut the squares on the big paper cutters.

Handmade papers cut into 11 inch circles to mount on the poster board.

Handmade papers are now available at many art stores at very reasonable prices. So it is worth looking around in your area for some good prices. You can make at least three circles from a sheet. The reason we like handmade papers for this is that they look beautiful on the poster board, with some of the color showing through from behind. I take my colored poster boards and put the papers on the background to see which ones I like the best. Beginning with a beautiful base makes a big difference in how much joy each person gets from this project and in how successful the project is.

Glue Sticks and Aleene's Tacky Glue

Patterned handmade papers

Tissue paper

Sequins, including stars and spirals

Ribbons of all colors and widths

Embroidery thread in lots of colors

Yarns with different textures and colors

Sparkling, delicate, gossamer-like thread

Thin wire of many different colors to decorate with or to use to attach beads, stones, or crystals

Beads of all kinds

Rocks and crystals

Seashells

Old jewelry and watch parts

Directions

When you are ready to begin each person can choose the color of the base they want and a precut circle or circles of paper to mount on it. Glue sticks work fine to mount the circles to the poster board.

Now they are ready to decorate their mandala based on the theme or themes you are using together.

Everything you can think of and can find in art stores, in your back yard, on the mountainside, by the ocean, in your collections of "stuff," and things you have used before for other projects is great for making and decorating the mandalas.

Because our "Body Now" cycle is a mandala (see the illustration on p. 45) we have often used the mandala's circular form as a way to decorate and symbolize and play our way through the healing cycle, spiraling into "The Body Now" at the center. Working with ancient and sacred symbols is always especially rich and this beautiful little project is no exception. Combined with movement and sharing and song, our participants have changed their entire sense of who they are—falling in love with their essence and their goodness.

Traditionally a ritual symbol that represents the universe, the mandala fits beautifully in our work, as we believe the universe is inside and outside our bodies and that it is always a source of deep loving energy.

Working in a circle also allows us to remember the repeating cycles of the earth, the moon, and of our bodies as we spiral through our lives, always evolving and learning.

This is too big a project for a one-hour break in the afternoon of a one-day workshop. It works best if you have least a three-day span and even better over a whole week or a series of weeks if you are doing a once-a-week format.

Themes
We have done this project concentrating on one quadrant each day, following the cycle of our healing mandala, starting with awakening and then moving on to embracing, loving, and acting. Some folks stayed in that form and others worked back and forth, moving between all the quadrants, while other just started, letting their intuition and body guide them through. It is all good.

Another time when I was working with a group of women over 60, we used the mandala project more like a timeline and moved through the stages of our lives, honoring our stories as we went from birth to future around the mandala.

We made self-love mandalas at one workshop, spending the whole week adding in symbols to remind us of things we really loved about ourselves, and new parts we wanted to honor, and new discoveries we made about our gifts.

Providing a structure helps some people get started; letting go of the structure is equally important for others. What matters is that we create a sacred, loving space for each person to explore their own journey around the mandala in ease and joy.

Group Art

Creating group art is a wonderful way to experience the power of collaboration and the fun of letting go of control. It releases everybody from the comparative mindset and from being focused on the finished product. Instead the process and relating to each other and inviting all the gifts in the group into the story becomes the focus, whether consciously or unconsciously.

Group Project Ideas

We have done group **collages**, where we all cut images from magazines and combine them on a big piece of paper that covers a whole section of the wall where you are meeting.

We have made one **wand** by passing it around a group and each person adds something. Each person can then take it home for a turn and then mail or deliver it to the next person.

We have made group **weavings** where we create a sort of dream catcher base and everybody adds on to it as the week goes on.

We have made **journals** where each person adds in their own writing, word game words (see p. 325), doodles, drawings, magazine pieces, strings, cut paper designs, and poetry until the whole book is filled with our group energy. Establishing a theme for the journal that matches your week or weeks together is helpful.

We have made **group poems** where each person writes one line that is their dream or wish for themselves or the world and the lines are then randomly combined into a poem.

We have made **group paintings**, where large sheets of butcher paper cover the wall, creating the canvas, and folks go back and forth between moving and adding color and shapes to the painting.

We have created eleven fully produced evening-length **performances** from a combination of everyone's stories and movements and songs, with as many as 15 artists collaborating on costumes, video, sets, choreography, songs, narrative, original music, and dance.

So the possibilities are endless and the rewards are great. As we create this new world together, co-creation is at the center of what will make it all come together and be sustainable. We might as well start practicing now.

Exercises

Calling Home

This is probably the most powerful community forming exercise we do. No matter how we begin, we always end in a connected and accepting place that is sustainable and transforming for all of us. Many different levels of our basic being and our basic goodness are touched with this ritual exercise.

Almost everybody who participates in this exercise experiences some shift in their sense of who they are and how they view others. It is always hard to separate from each other at the end, as we have connected on a deep, vibrational level. We often use this to end a workshop or at the end of a series of classes, and it can be a powerful way to begin as well.

Every time I do this exercise, my trust in the basic goodness of humanity is deepened and reinforced. The story here is the group story. It is the story of people sinking down into their bodies and their hearts and their intuitive, loving, accepting selves, and hanging out there long enough to experience how different that feels on every level of their being. It is the story of people creating a new reference point for how it can feel to be alive. It is about people creating new possibilities and new stories for themselves and the people in their circle.

Directions

You can use the script below, in italics, to guide a group through this exercise.

We are going to divide up into two groups. Most of the group will go to one side of the room and three to five participants will go to the other side. Stay close now, though, while I explain what we are doing.

This activity is called, "Calling Home." The large group is going to represent "home," for this exercise. The small group on this side of the room is going to start. They will be the ones who are traveling home to their own authentic story. Everyone will get a turn. We will just keep feeding you all into the smaller group from the larger group as we go.

One person from the small group is going to stand up and face the small group with her back to the large group. She (or he) is going to close her eyes and move slowly backwards toward the group on the other side of the room. The group that she is leaving will send her off by surrounding her with loving sounds of support and care, sounds to support her in taking her journey.

When s/he is about one fourth of the way across the room, those sounds will fade away as the group on the other side of the room begins to make sounds of calling her home. That group is going to reflect her pace and her movements in sound, affirming who she is in this moment, calling her home to herself.

We will only make sounds, being sure to leave any words or phrases out, as they would carry meaning that could be distracting for our traveler.

With her eyes closed, the person who is traveling across the room navigates by sound and energy. She is finding her way with the help of both groups, one which begins by sending her off on her journey, and then one that welcomes her home. She can go slow or fast, walk or dance wildly, or anything she likes during her crossing.

Sarah will be spotting her the whole time, walking along with her on the side, making sure she is safe.

When she reaches home, the group will gently fold her in, letting her drop into their arms and their sound, gently holding her as she opens her eyes and emerges back into the room. Then she will join that group and help sound and guide the next person across.

If it is your turn to come across and you are feeling scared, you can ask somebody to go with you and hold your hand, and keep you safe as you go across the room. Or, you can start with your eyes open, and close them when you feel comfortable and then open them again if you want to. This seems a little scary when we talk about it, but it is really fun to do, and once you do it you will want to do it again. So, take your time and really have your turn.

Sarah and I will sound with you so that sounders know what to do, and we will also spot you so that you are totally safe. Okay? Let's try it. Who would like to go first on this side of the room? Great, Lizzi. Stand here facing me and close your eyes. As we surround you with our loving sound, focus for a moment on how amazing and wonderful you are just like you are right now. Take a deep breath as you begin.

Remember, everyone, keep your sounds loving and comforting as you send Lizzi off and as you call her home.

Facilitation Suggestions

Make sure the large group is clumped closely together, so their sound will be focused and so they can catch the mover coming in. Have someone you can count on help the receiving group take the mover in with care.

Stand with the group that is letting someone go. Begin to sound, sweetly and gently, sounds of releasing. You can cue the group on the other side of the room to begin sounding when the mover is about one fourth of the way across the room, until they get the hang of it. They will probably start on their own, which is great. The receiving group should get quiet again at the start of the next person's journey.

It is important to remind your group that we are only making sounds, and not using words or phrases.

Have one person always spotting your mover, physically guiding her if she needs it. You, or a helper, will need to be on the other side, so you can keep feeding people into the smaller group. Bring two to three people from the larger group into the smaller one at a time but do this quietly to avoid distractions. You don't want a long pause between movers so the energy doesn't drop.

You and the musician and the sounders are creating a sacred space with sound in this exercise. Try to give as many directions at the beginning as you can so that you don't have to interrupt the mood.

When a group is mostly finished crossing and there are only one or two people left to go across, some of your folks who have already gone across can come over and help with sounding for the last few participants.

If you have a co-leader or a helper, have her or him sound with the receiving group and help you spot that side. Then you can focus on helping people get started smoothly and help keep people moving through. Also, if people want to go across with a partner, your helper can partner with them.

When you are spotting, don't be afraid to get right in there and take someone's shoulders in order to prevent them from getting hurt. It is much better to startle a person by touching them than to let them crash into something or someone.

If the group as a whole seems to be scared, or if you have a very large group, you may want to have two or three people go across at the same time. Spotting is trickier and more important in this case, but it generally works quite well. You may need one person on each side

You can do many variations on this exercise if fear is an issue for your group or for individuals. There are a lot of options, from participants keeping their eyes open all the way across to eight people holding hands in a chain as they walk backwards across the room.

Centering

Many of us go through our lives quite disconnected from our bodies and breath: off center, rushing around, reaching and contracting, unconsciously trying to find a place that makes sense or feels balanced and workable. Most of us don't have a daily practice, like meditation or yoga or authentic movement that consistently returns us to our center point. This simple exercise, though certainly not a substitute for a mediation practice, is an amazing little "quick fix" when you and your participants need to get centered. It never fails to improve the situation, whatever it is. This is also a really effective exercise to use after a name circle to help a group get grounded and present for the class. It is a very nurturing and focused exercise that doesn't get the participants stuck in an internal state.

In one workshop we had a particularly large group of people performing, with a broad range of ages including thirteen children. It was a wonderfully enthusiastic and committed group, and a very hard group to keep focused. In one especially rowdy rehearsal, I was beginning to get a little overwhelmed and cranky. Our very high energy six-year-old came over to me, got me to kneel down, and whispered in my ear that maybe we all needed to do that earth and sky exercise, because things seemed to be a little noisy.

Of course we did what she suggested, and it worked like magic.

Directions

You can use the script below, in italics, to guide a group through this exercise.

Begin in a circle.

Everyone take a deep breath and sigh out loud…. Do that again with your eyes closed this time… and drop your breath down into your feet. Feel all your energy drop right down through your body and into your feet that are being supported by the floor and by the earth below it.

And now, keeping your feet where they are, just let your body begin to sway gently forward and back, forward and back. Play with your weight shifting from your toes to your heels and let that get bigger and bigger until you are moving as far forward as you can and as far backward as you can without falling over. Then slowly let that get smaller and smaller and smaller, very gradually, until you can hardly even sense that you are moving forward and back. Breathe and let your jaw relax. Feel that little shift from front to back that keeps you standing upright.

Now slowly begin to shift from right to left, gradually making that bigger and bigger, just gently falling from one side to the other. When that is as big as it can be, begin to make it a little smaller and then a little smaller than that, gradually shifting smaller and smaller until you can just feel a tiny inner shift from one side to the other. Breathe and relax here for a moment, and just notice the little shift from left to right working with that shift from front to back, allowing you to keep your balance.

Now let your weight fall to the front, to the right, to the back, and to the left, making a circle. Keep feeling your feet in one place on the floor, breathe, and let that circle get bigger and bigger until you can't get it any bigger without losing your balance. When you have found that limit, that edge, slowly begin making your circles smaller and smaller, circling and spiraling into the center of your body until you spiral right into your moving center. Feel that spiral going through the middle of your body, a sort of crystalline energy spiraling and moving and connecting up into the sky and down into the earth. Feel the line of energy that drops from the sky straight through the core of your body down into the center of the earth, with your energy spiraling around it.

Take a deep breath, and slowly blink your eyes open towards the floor. Begin moving slowly in the space from that place of balance and clear center, just letting your body follow your relaxed, breathing center around the room.

Facilitation Suggestions

I always start the spiral falling to the front. I have noticed that it can throw people off balance to start to the back or the side.

Talk about the connection between earth and sky to center and balance people at the end. If you do it at the beginning it feels confusing to the body—too many directions—but at the end it makes sense and helps people come to balance and get ready to move.

This exercise works wonders if you have a group that is a little rowdy and out of their bodies or a group that is tired or stressed. It is also wonderful before a performance. It is a great way for people to collect themselves and come into their bodies.

Acknowledgement

I learned a version of this exercise forty years ago from a track coach in high school. He taught it to us to help us deal with anxiety before competitions. I am sure it made a big difference in our performance. He was ahead of his time. Thank you Cherry Creek High School track coach 1961!

Copy Circle

This circle is a good way to begin the process of relating to each person's goodness and to practice accepting everyone as they are. We get to see them, to reflect them, and to affirm them exactly as they are in that moment. It is healing for the person being reflected and for each person in the group. It is a kind of simple ritual circle, a home base that brings the group back to just being and seeing and moving together.

The exercise gives everyone a chance to be the leader, and equally important, gives each participant an opportunity to follow every other person in the circle. A lot of seeing and affirming of each other gets done on a body level, with almost no stress. In addition, a copy circle is a great way to bring everyone back together as a final exercise in your class. It also works well as a transition in the middle of a class to reconnect everybody and ground them before beginning a new exercise.

One little girl in a copy circle in Iowa didn't want to lead when it came to her turn in the circle. She smiled kind of shyly and shook her head no. I was getting ready to jump in and say that's fine, you can always pass if you want to, when the group began smiling and shaking their heads. She loved being reflected and shook her head even harder and then very, very slowly she put her hands over her face and laughed and laughed. The group just followed along and then the next person in line took over and let her off the hook. Later in the class when we did another copy circle, she jumped right in and took her turn. It was such a beautiful example of the power of group wisdom. I count on it.

Directions

You can use the script below, in italics, to guide a group through this exercise.

Take people's hands and gather them together into a circle. Stay in motion, keep the music going, and when everyone is there, begin doing a repetitive movement. Talk over the music.

Everyone follow me. Just do what I do at the same time as I do it. Remember to modify any of the movements if you need to, so they work for your body and your energy level.

Give them a moment to catch on and begin following you. Then demonstrate for them.

And when I'm ready, I'll pass it on to Tanja and we will all follow her.

Literally pass the movement as if you were passing her a plate or a ball, or make any gesture that communicates "your turn." The group will follow along and begin following the next person and the next. Everyone moves simultaneously, being led by person after person around the circle. Guide them through with words as they go, talking over the music.

Move however you want to right now, the music will follow you. We will all follow you. When you are finished, pass it on to the next person.

Facilitation Suggestions

Always remind participants that when they are copying they can modify the movement any way they want to make it comfortable and safe for their bodies.

A good way to bring the group together for this is to just start taking people's hands as they are completing an exercise. Just put out your hands and get a few people connected and the rest will follow.

Sometimes people won't have heard or understood the directions, or they'll get caught up in following or leading. If someone doesn't seem to know what is happening, just guide him or her right in the moment, like:

Andy, we're following you, now.

Rick, pass the lead to Linda as soon as you are ready.

If you are pressed for time at the end of a class let them know that: *We are going to do a fast copy circle today, because we are almost out of time, so let's keep it moving quickly around the circle.*

Finding a Fit

What do I want?	What is needed that I can give?

How do these go together?

Journey to Joy

What do you like to do in the morning?

What makes you smile when you are doing it?

When do you think you are just having fun, not working?

What makes you feel energized and alive?

What flows effortlessly for you?

What do your dreams tell you that you love?

What do you imagine a lot?

What do you often wish for in your life?

What do you like to do in the evening?

What brings up a full body "yes" for you? ("Yes, Yes, Yes!")

Leading Blind and Sculpting

This is a loving and transforming exercise that works on many levels and can be counted on to transform your group into a community. It addresses issues of leadership, trust, connection, and group awareness. It works best with groups of mixed ages.

It is equally profound to play either role in the exercise, either to let someone else decide your shape, or to take the initiative to create an experience for someone else. Once the group has done this together, they see each other differently and dance together with a different level of awareness and connection.

I am always surprised at how much this exercise changes group dynamics, even when I least expect it. We had a group of people with very diverse socioeconomic backgrounds in Massachusetts, with the added mix of several participants who were mentally and physically challenged. The groups had managed to stay pretty separated in the warm up, which doesn't usually happen, so I wasn't sure how they would do with this exercise. We jumped in anyway and watched the room magically transform before our eyes.

All the differences dropped away and the group became one big beautiful moving organism. They were able to connect much more easily with the pace of the class slowed down. The fast and energetic warm ups were more threatening for this group than the slower, more intimate form.

Directions

You can use the script below, in italics, to guide a group through this exercise.

Everyone find a partner. One of you is going to close your eyes and your partner is going to lead you gently and slowly around the room. When you are the leader, your job is to keep your partner safe at all times, so choose a way to guide her that feels secure. For instance, I could lead with one arm around my partner's waist and the other holding her hand. Or, I could lead by facing her and holding both her hands as I walk backwards and she walks forwards. Both ways, I have enough contact with my partner to keep her safe.

Demonstrate both of these ways of leading.

If you are being led and you want to open your eyes and then close them again, that is fine, or if you want to keep your eyes open while you are being led, that is fine too. Take care of yourself and do what feels comfortable to you.

Decide who will lead first. Everybody ready? Begin slowly and carefully leading your partner around the room. I will tell you when to switch leaders. See if you can keep your eyes closed so that you feel what it is like to be led, or blur your eyes and let your focus be inside.

Let the pairs walk around the room for about a minute.

Now, switch who is leading and do the same thing.

Let the pairs walk around the room again for about a minute.

Now go back to your original leader, and this time, you are going to lead your partner to a new place in the room and then stop and make a sculpture by placing your partner in a shape. Your partner will stand with her eyes closed, and you will move her into a shape by placing her hands and arms where you want them, maybe gently moving her head, turning her upper body, bending her knees slightly, moving a foot forward, and so on.

Demonstrate this while you are explaining.

Then you will leave her in that shape, and she will stay still while you go on to find another statue in the room whose position you want to change. So, at this point, half of the people in the room will be sculptures, and half will be making sculptures.

If you are making a sculpture, be really careful to touch people appropriately and gently. Treat them with care. It is a gift that they are allowing you to move their bodies. And if you are the one being sculpted, remember that you can open your eyes at any time. If someone puts you in a position that is uncomfortable or hard to hold, go right ahead and change it. Don't do anything you don't want to do. Let's begin and I will talk you through the rest.

Have really sweet music playing. The mood of this exercise is reverent and calm, sweet and loving. After a few minutes the partners will switch roles.

Whenever you want to, you can switch roles. If you have been made into a sculpture, go ahead and move out of your stillness and begin sculpting someone else. And if you have been doing the sculpting, come to stillness and close your eyes and wait. Someone will come and lead you to a new place and begin sculpting you. Try both roles if you wish.

You can also connect the person you are leading to another still person. Just keep quietly working together, moving and sculpting, and waiting in stillness.

Let them play with this for a little while. Watch the room carefully. Remind them to take care of themselves at all times. If you see that a person is uncomfortable, remind everyone that they can change their positions whenever they want, open their eyes, or change roles.

Now, as you are moving through the room, begin to connect people to each other, or find a place to connect yourself, so that eventually the whole group is formed into one connected sculpture.

Let that sculpture resolve into stillness and then transition into a sounding circle, or just let them all be still for a few moments and then have everyone take a deep breath, blink their eyes open, and begin to look around and see each other in the sculpture.

Facilitation Suggestions
The first few steps of this exercise need to be explained before anyone tries them. People can feel very vulnerable during this one and need to have all of the options before they begin.

Once the group has begun the sculpting part of the exercise, then you should talk them through the rest of the exercise as they are moving. This way you can create a mood and keep everyone going within it. The mood is a very important part of the healing quality of the exercise.

You will need to have an even number of people for this exercise. It doesn't work in trios. So, you may need to facilitate and participate at the same time at the beginning, or have your assistant drop out for the first round. Once the group begins sculpting, you can stop being a participant because no one is paired anymore at this point.

If someone seems uncomfortable or is having trouble, quietly make a suggestion to the whole moving group, like "open your eyes and look around if you need to," or "remember that you can change your own shape if you want to." Don't single the person out or address him personally. Make all your suggestions to the group so that no one feels like he or she is doing it "wrong."

Acknowledgement

I first did the two parts of this exercise as separate pieces when I was a Camp Fire Girl. More recently, I played with these ideas with both Liz Lerman and Nancy Spanier.

Letting Go of the Mother's Breath
Becoming Breathtaking!

What do you remember seeing on your mother's dresser when you were a child?

What do you remember seeing in your mother's purse when you were a child?

What do you remember about your mother's hair when you were a child?

What do you remember your mother saying about herself?

What do you remember hearing your mother say to others in the family?

What do you remember hearing your mother say about others?

What do you remember your mother saying to you that felt good?
My mother loved my...

My mother always…

I could trust my mother to…

What are some of the things you would like to
appreciate your mother for and thank her for giving you?
In gratitude and love I thank you, Mom, for…

What do wish your mom would have done or been like?

I wish my mom had…

My mother would never….

My mother hated to….

My mother was afraid ….

What are the things you would like to give back to your
mother?
In gratitude and respect, Mom, I give you back…

Name Dance

My real name is

My name once was

My heart says my name is

In my dreams my name is

Secretly I know my name is

Tomorrow my name will be

Right now my name is

Seed

The seed exercise is at the core of Turning the Wheel's search for experiences that are completely authentic in their expression and that celebrate and encourage our differences, while creating a sense of the cohesive group. Each person gets to shine in his or her own moment, and the group gets to shine in response. This form, which has been universally fun for every group we have worked with, plays with the tension and the excitement that lies along the meeting point of the individual and the group, the leader and the follower.

When Barbara Dilley first introduced her form of this exercise, she presented it as an opportunity for solo work, which it certainly is. I think it seduces us with that wonderful chance to be seen for as long as we want, until we decide to stop. We get to lead, to be in charge: to make our own choices.

As the other steps—the group responding and the creation of the still sculpture—are added, the process quietly layers on all those lessons of seeing the other person just as they are, responding attentively to that picture, and then pausing to be "in the moment" of that reflection. The stillness at the end is as important to our body learning as the moving is at the beginning.

This exercise is a great place for facilitators to play with adapting their process to the group. It can be done so many ways and still be fun and look great. In Wyoming, we had one woman who couldn't make up her mind about which shape to take, and where to join the sculpture. She just kept changing and moving and almost stopping and then moving again. It was a beautiful performance piece on "authentic indecision." It was very humorous, and very familiar to all of us. It gave us an idea for a whole different form of this exercise where half of the group would make a solid sculpture and the other half would try on all different responses to that shape. The groups took turns being the still folks and the movers.

Directions

You can use the script below, in italics, to guide a group through this exercise.

Start with everyone standing in a circle.

For this exercise, one person goes in the middle of the circle and makes a shape. You can take your time dancing in the middle before you take your shape, or you might simply run in and strike a pose. Then, as soon as that "seed" person is totally still, the rest of the group is going to run in and take a shape in response to the seed shape and get very still. Together, everyone makes one big, still sculpture. Hold the shape until the seed person moves.

Do an example or two, talking the group through the exercise so they get a feel for it. Cue them as to when to rush in and when to back away. Try to use your tone of voice to inspire focus and quiet. If they've got the hang of it, add in the next step.

Now play with different ways of responding to the seed person. You can play with different levels, using the floor or towering over the seed person.

You can run in and be really close to the seed person, or you could try being far away from her or turned away.

Demonstrate this while you are talking, teaching by your example.

Repeat the exercise over and over with different "seed" people. Give everyone a chance to be the "seed." If someone is having trouble taking a turn, they usually will go with a friend or with the facilitator.

Facilitation Suggestions
Once you have taught the exercise in a large group, it is nice to break into smaller groups, like eight or ten people, so that each person gets a turn to be the "seed" more frequently. Once people get over their initial fear, they usually want as many turns as they can get. You need a co-leader or helper for each group.

Breaking into smaller groups also means you can take turns watching each other do about three of the seed sculptures. This is a really good way for the members of the group to get new ideas, to see what they like, and to practice appreciating each other. Be sure to appreciate and clap for each group after they perform for the class.

A fun next step with this exercise is to create a continuous sculpture, where the group stays still in the sculpture until somebody moves. Then they all move into a new shape, which makes a new sculpture, and they hold that one until somebody moves again. The exercise makes a beautiful changing sculpture, alternating between moving and stillness, seamlessly, with no apparent stopping and starting cue.

The continuous sculpture exercise above can be too confusing for some groups, never knowing when to be still or when to move. A good interim step or alternative we originally created for a group of kids in Massachusetts was to have them make a sculpture and hold the shape until the musician played. Then they would move with the music, and freeze when the music stopped. That freeze would create the new sculpture. This was fun and easy for everybody. Our musicians played all kinds of rhythms and sounds, including tongue clicking, whistling, singing, flutes, bouzouki (lute), drums, and piano, so the kids had the added experience of moving to all kinds of music, and even broadening their definition of music.

This exercise works as well for kids as for adults, and it is great for people with physical or mental challenges. We use it with elders in the nursing homes who have to stay in their wheelchairs. They move and respond right from where they are sitting in their chairs. When working with kids, the main challenge is to get them to quiet themselves and focus at the start. Once they tune in, they usually stay engaged, especially if the circle is small enough (six to eight people) that they each get a turn relatively often. It helps to challenge them to see how still and quiet they can be.

If people are shy about going into the circle by themselves, offer to go with them or urge them to go in with a friend or friends. Be creative with ways to urge them to try it, but remember that no one has to go in if they don't want to. Usually someone else in the group will convince the person to go in with her or him.

When we are working with kids or having trouble with physical boundaries, we sometimes need to make the whole process slower, and we give them these parameters:

1. *We don't touch the seed person so they feel safe when they take their shape.*

2. *We don't make gestures of violence towards any person.* (We let them make them fists or other gestures towards the floor, the ceiling, or the wall if they seem to need to do that, just not towards any person.)

Once you make these parameters clear, be sure to watch the group and remind people of the parameters if they are acting outside of them.

Human Machine Variation

The Human Machine is a fun variation on the "Seed" exercise that appeals to adults and children alike. Have one person go into the middle of the circle and do a repeating movement and repeating sound. Have five or six people join that person, one at a time, adding their own repetitive movement and sound.

When all seven people are in the middle together making their movements and sounds, you can cue them to have their machine slow down and stop. When the group has done a few of these, play with having people leave the machine when they are ready, and having others join in so that the machine never stops but it is always changing.

Sometimes our youth like to choose a machine to create and then see what happens, like a bubble gum machine or a computer machine.

Acknowledgement
We adapted this from a solo work exercise that I learned from Barbara Dilley.

Sounding Circle

This exercise is a beautiful way to end a class or workshop, and we end almost every one we teach with a sounding circle or a song. By bringing everyone's energy together for one last moment of relating in community, it creates a sense of unity and trust. And, because people are encouraged to be contributing members of the group and at the same time to be aware of others, it provides another opportunity to balance self-expression with community awareness.

Most of all, it is very grounding and centering, which is good for people before they go back out in the world. The songs that are created in these closing circles can be so beautiful that you can hardly bear to hear them. They are the culmination of a whole class of connecting, seeing, and sharing, and that is often reflected in the sensitivity of this last moment.

A young girl in Nova Scotia who had spent the week dancing with us started crying during the sounding circle. The group held her in their sound and energy until the circle closed, but everybody was clearly worried about her. I think we were afraid the intensity was too much for one so young. When we asked her if she was okay, she said she was just so filled with feelings from the week of dancing that it was overflowing. She said it was almost as good as going to church, a compliment, I think.

Directions

You can use the script below, in italics, to guide a group through this exercise.

Gather the group in a tight circle. Have everyone stand shoulder to shoulder or put their arms around each other's waists.

Close your eyes and take a deep breath and gently sigh out loud.

Do that again one more time and this time let the sound keep coming at the end of your sigh. Now let your voice make any sound you want as you listen to the other sounds around you, blending and reflecting and listening and sounding your own sound.

Keeping your eyes closed, if you are comfortable with that, just keep toning, changing tones whenever you want. Keep going and let your sounds become single sustained tones, breathing whenever you need to, and changing to new tone whenever you wish.

See if you can hear every other sound in the circle while making your own sound.

Listening and toning, toning and listening, we are creating our closing song for tonight.

The toning will last for a little while. Usually the group will bring the sounding to a close without any cue from you. The group seems to know when to close together. If you have to end before they are ready you can just gently talk them to a close.

And now, slowly let your sound fade away.

Let the circle come to silence and stay that way for a few seconds. Then help them shift their focus from internal to external.

Deep breath, everyone.

Blink your eyes open toward the floor and see all the toes in the circle, and shoes and socks.

See each other. Let your eyes connect with each other to help you come fully back into your body. Thank each other with your eyes for being here to dance today.

Thank the musician.

One final piece we do to close the sound circle, which you could do if you wish, is to all put our arms above our heads, reaching up into the sky, sending love out to whoever needs it. Then we share some love around the circle by wiggling our hands at each other, and take some love in for ourselves before dropping to touch the floor, to ground ourselves into the earth, while saying, "touch the earth, dance forever." This usually turns into a moment of fun hand drumming on the floor.

Facilitation Suggestions

Don't be afraid to give directions during the sounding. If you have a noisy group you could start by telling them to be careful of each other's ears since we are so close to each other. If someone is making painfully loud sounds, you can gently remind the group to listen to every other sound in the circle while making their own sound.

When you begin speaking over the group's sounding, it helps to begin your suggestions with words like:

Keep your sounds going, and...

That way they don't stop sounding altogether. This is also nice because it challenges them again to sound and listen at the same time.

Acknowledgement
We imported this exercise from women's ritual circles.

Spaces Between

We live in a culture that is driven and contracted and stressed most of the time. Many of us don't even know what our bodies feel like when they are truly released and flowing with easy strength. Even when we sleep we are often worried and tense. So much of our dis-ease is rooted in this stress, and many of our elders are paying the price for a life lived in contraction. On some simple level, I feel like this exercise and others like it are crucial to our overall well-being and happiness.

This sequence is a blending of Body Mind Centering studies, Ruth Zaporah, and all of my training in releasing as the key to power and sustained strength, whether in dancing, or raising children, or building dreams. It is a slow and gentle warm-up that leaves your participants ready to move on all levels.

Some time ago, one of our dancers in Colorado came into the room unable to move because of a back and hip injury. She started this exercise on a mat in the middle of the room and by the end was up moving around with the whole group.

Contracting around the pain was making the injuries much more painful and immobilizing. During the discussion at the end of the exercise, an older woman said that she had never moved so freely in her life as she did today, and she thought the exercise had put spaces between the sorrow in her life and the contraction around her heart. We feel so grateful for the gift of these courageous people who yield to the possibility of change and are willing to take the risk of being fully present in the moment.

Directions

You can use the script below, in italics, to guide a group through this exercise.

Have each person find a space in the room that feels like their starting place. This exercise is a very individual exploration at the beginning and then reconnects everybody at the end.

Begin by taking a deep breath and releasing it with a noisy sigh, lots of sound. Do that one more time. Feel your feet on the floor and your jaw released. Let your breath be easy.

Begin walking in the space and focusing on your bones, your skeleton. Play with the idea that you are just a set of bones with fluids around them moving in the space. Imagine all of those bones floating apart, releasing any stress between them, and letting the fluids pour into those spaces between, soothing and lubricating your bones.

Feel your pelvis as a floating bowl with your legs just floating loose out of this easy floating pelvis, and your spine floating up out of that pelvis, loose and easy, just floating up through space with your head bobbing comfortably around on top of the spine.

Release your jaw and your belly and let your breath be easy.

Focus on your spine again and let the vertebrae float apart, opening up space between each one so the fluids can rush in and release the spine to an easy fluid movement.

Let your legs float loosely out of your easy pelvis and feel the space between your hip joint and the top of your leg. Let fluids pour in and release that connection, so it is floating free and released. Feel your legs just floating loose in space, not connected to your pelvis, just floating free out of a floating pelvis.

Let the bones in your knees float apart and open up, with space between the leg bones and the knee bones. The whole leg is floating apart and lots of space is opening up all down through the leg and into the ankle.

If you feel a tight spot anywhere in the leg, open up space for the fluids to come in and release the tension.

Let the anklebones open up and float apart, and feel the foot release into the floor as the ankle opens up and floats free. Feel the bones in your toes and your feet pull apart and let the spaces between them fill up with fluids. Move around in space feeling the fluid, released movement of your feet and your ankles as they provide an easy, open, moving base for your whole body.

Move around in the space now with these released easy feet and legs floating out of a floating released pelvis with a spine flowing easily up into the space and let the shoulder connections open up and float apart creating those spaces again for the fluids to pour in. Move down your arms and let the elbows open up and the bones in the arms separate from the elbows. Feel the elbows open and easy, able to float free.

Let all the little bones in your wrists and your hands open up and relax into a fluid energy, with no stress or tension in them. Let the

287

hand float away from the wrists and do their own dance of release and space. Feel your knuckles open up and separate from your fingertips, letting them all drop into fluid relaxation.

Keep moving in the space, allowing all of these released parts to breathe and dance and play with each other.

Feel your head floating free above the spine as the bones at the top of the spine open up to release your head. Fluids rush in and bathe the tired joints in back of the neck, releasing the tension and allowing the joints to float free.

The plates in the head open up making room for the brain and for all the fluids in the brain to breathe and relax and let go for a few moments. Feel the brain stretching and releasing and floating around inside these open and released plates of your head. Let the fluids rush in behind your eyes, and around your ears and into the joints of your jaw.

Take this released and fluid body out into the space more. Move a little faster, feeling the power and strength in this release. Notice the space between the top of your head and your pelvis, between your fingers and your toes, between your chest and your knees.

As you begin to move a little more, see the spaces between you and others in the room. See if you can keep this open flowing body with you and begin to see and respond to the people moving in the room with you. If you feel a contraction or a tightening, just focus on that point and put some space in, open up a place for the fluids to flow in.

Try moving a little more quickly in the space and making small jumps from this place of release. Play with the power you can access from release. Experiment with changing the spaces between you and the others in the room. Make choices from this easy place about how close or far you want to be from the others.

Keep moving and breathing. Find a partner and do a "spaces between" duet. See if you can move with your partner from this place of open, easy access and gentle released connection. Just play together, sometimes copying each other, sometimes responding to each other.

You may have times of stillness, move quickly, or move very slowly. Just keep coming back to releasing and breathing and letting your power come from this open energy.

Let the group members dance with their partners for a few minutes and then cue them to find the end of this "spaces between" dance.

Have them take a few minutes to talk to their partners about that experience and get a drink before you bring them back together. This is a long exercise. It is helpful for participants to have a break and a little time to share with another person.

Facilitation Suggestions

You can use a little piece of this in any of the warm up exercises. Just remind people to breathe and open up spaces between their bones for the fluids to rush in. This works especially well if they have experienced this more complex version sometime before.

This is a long process and works best with a group that has been working on their movement and their body awareness with you for a while. It takes quite a bit of commitment to stay focused all the way through. It is also fine to do a shortened version by not being so detailed in the visualization.

As in many other exercises like this, your voice needs to be gentle and easy, unhurried and unworried. Dancers will work with this at their own level, so it helps to not have any preset expectations. Gently guide them through and let them see what they discover. Each time I do this I find something new.

Acknowledgement
Body Mind Centering, Ruth Zaporah, Eloise Ristad, and Elaine Yarbrough.

Spiraling Into "The Body Now"

Our model for moving into joy and self-love is a four-step mandala of healing, called "The Body Now." (See illustration p. 45.) It is an improvisational movement-based journey to our essence that is an ongoing process of evolving with ease and love. Once you get started on the mandala, you just keep spiraling into more and more embodied joy. There is no beginning or end. You can enter at any point on the circle and have an immediate new beginning. The magic is in the willingness to make the first move, to actually step into well-being -- being well. The brain will quickly rewire your system for this new choice and then keep rewiring as you continue to make new choices that move you deeper into your own authentic story.

Spontaneous expression of any kind will send you back into your limitless "yes" reality. Just choose any of the activities listed below, which were generated by workshop participants, or add your favorite activity and go for it. It only takes the first step or even a small gesture in your body and your brain will take you the rest of the way home. Just drop into your body in your favorite way and move yourself into ease and joy.

The exciting thing about getting moving is that you can just spiral right to the middle of the "The Body Now" mandala and you are home without doing any processing, changing your past, analyzing, suffering, or fixing of yourself.

This list is just a beginning of some of the ways we can keep moving. You can add your own and keep adding new ones every week as you discover new fun ways to get in your body.

The key is: **Express, Express, Express!**

Move and Sound and Breathe

This is the catch-all for those of you who don't want any specific directions, and it is a fast track into the center of the mandala.

Just start moving around any way want and make any sound that comes out of your knowing body and the breath will follow. Music that you love can help you get started. You are guaranteed to be fully in "The Body Now" within 10 minutes of moving and sounding, with an added bonus of a fresh and open perspective on everything.

Breathe

Breathe into your feet.

Breathe from your belly.

Breathe all the way out and find your reflex breath.

Move

Improvisational Dance

Move any way you want, letting your body lead.

Move from your bones, your heart, your breath, your fluids, your organs, your feet, or just follow your thumb around the room.

Just be you, moving around the room, enjoying yourself. Drop into a dreamy space and float around in your dreams.

Listen to a visualizations in this book online at (www.turningthewheel.org/audio) and dance with your fluids, in your garden, or commune with the stars.

Be a ballerina, a hip-hop dude or dudette, a rock-out disco diva, a creative movement genius, a jazz extremist, or an African ritual dancer.

Look at our book *Dancing Our Way Home* to see hundreds of ways to improvise and play in movement. (Available on amazon.com or at turningthewheel.org.)

Exercise

Walk anywhere.

Walk in nature.

Walk fast.

Walk slow.

Take a long hike.

Play with a hula hoop.

Bike.

Swim.

Climb.

Run up and down the stairs.

Workout at home.

Go to the gym and workout.

Go for a run.

Go rollerblading, ice skating, roller skating.

Throw or kick a ball.

Swing on a swing.

Play tag.

Just run around. (My granddaughter's favorite thing to do.)

Lay on the Earth

Listen to the sounds of the earth and gently move with those sounds.

Hug Yourself

Gently rub your arms and legs and chest and back, feeling the edges of your body.

Ask someone to hold you.

Ask someone to rock you.

Vocalize

Sing a song.

Make whatever sounds come bubbling up: sustained tones, staccato sounds, high or low sounds, animal or nature sounds, etc.

Chant: pick a phrase to repeat over and over and let your body respond in movement.

Feel your Feelings

Reveal/share your feelings while moving any way your body decides to move.

Listen consciously to yourself or a friend.

Turn Your Attention Toward Yourself

See an open space for yourself and move into it.

Turn your attention toward your heart.

Be grateful for one thing.

Appreciate Yourself or Appreciate Someone Else

See "Appreciations" (p. 38).

Laugh and Laugh

Go to Your Special Place and Find Silence

Write in Your Journal

Change the position of your body often as you write.

Meditate

See "Morning Practices" (p. 77) for discussion of these meditation options.

Improvised Meditation
Walking Meditation
Standing Meditation
Lying Down

Get a Snack

Take a Nap

Create Something

Paint a rock.
Wrap a rock with colored string.
Draw, doodle, scribble.
Sculpt.
Cut and glue.

Make a collage with paper, beads, paint,
found objects, words, or
magazine images.

Paint a picture.

Play with beads.

See "Art Projects" (p. 232) for other ideas.

Ongoing Paths

Build something, like a boat or a musical instrument.

Be in a performance.

Take a movement or dance class.

Take a drawing or painting or beading class.

Take a drumming class.

Join a nature walk or hiking group.

Join an exercise class.

Switching Places in the Circle

The beginning is such a crucial point in any class, as most people make up their minds very quickly about whether or not a class is a safe place to be. If they get a confused signal at the start, it is very difficult to change their perception.

This is how we begin most of our classes, and no matter which group of people we are working with, it seems to always work its magic. The group starts moving right away, with almost no directions. The exercise gets silly and playful easily and quickly, and it helps release the tension that exists when a group first comes into the circle. It's a great icebreaker for them and for you.

Directions

You can use the script below, in italics, to guide a group through this exercise.

Begin the class with everyone standing in a circle.

Everyone change places in the circle, all at the same time.

Do it yourself, and the group will follow.

Change places again. Keep going. Every time you see the circle start to take form, change places again.

Talk over the group as they are changing and moving and laughing and talking.

You can do this any way you want. You can cross right through the middle, or if you don't want to be in the crowd, go around the outside. You can move one step to the side, or you can stay where you are and the circle will change around you.

Wait until you see that the circle is almost formed again, and then change it. You can go fast, or you can go very slowly. You can go on the ground, or with a friend, or have a little interaction with someone as you go across.

Watch the group and call out whatever directions they need to keep going and stay relaxed.

If you are getting tired, go very, very slowly and see how that feels. Try being still in the middle and feel all the activity around you.

If someone is doing something you haven't thought of, then call that out to the group as an option. This will affirm their freedom of choice and their creativity.

You might want to try going across backwards like Gillian, or scooting across the floor like Tom.

Do a little dance in the middle like Sarah and Rosie if you want.

Add sound like Kathleen is doing. Sounds are always good. They help your body get warm.

Do this until the group is ready to transition into the next exercise.

Facilitation Suggestions

Teach this one by doing it yourself. Use your own big energy to get the group going. Start by doing simple crossings so they get the idea, and then add in some fun variations. They will catch on quickly.

Right at the start, be sure to give the group lots of "safe" options, like going around the outside or standing still, so they don't feel any pressure to be more athletic or more outgoing than they feel in that moment.

If people are struggling with the exercise or hesitating, sometimes more specific directions will get them going.

Try crossing the circle being as big as you possibly can. Be huge. Make huge sounds.

Now try sneaking across the circle. How invisible can you be? What does your body need to do to get very small and not be seen? Sneak around each other as if you are really hidden. How little can you get?

Now get really big again, noisy and obvious.

We usually use this exercise first and then follow with some form of game for learning names. The two together are a good combination to help people relax and feel safe.

In a nursing home where the whole group is unable to move to different places easily, we sometimes do this as a group for them, running around them and in front of them and behind them. The fun is contagious and they love to watch. It helps them relax, and get the idea of who we are.

Touching Lightly

This exercise is a very guided structure that involves a lot of physical contact. It is a safe and contained way to take people to a second step of contact dancing. It is deceptively intimate, without being scary. It quietly plays with issues of connection, boundaries, and separation on a body level, and it eases participants into contact dancing in a very safe way. It holds many elements of relating in one simple sequence and leaves us a little wiser even if we don't notice. We have had people develop long-term friendships that began with this exercise.

Directions

You can use the script below, in italics, to guide a group through this exercise.

Have everyone find a partner.

Move with your partner as close as you can to each other without touching. Start out slowly, exploring how close you can get. Try changing levels, try slowing down, and speeding up. One of you might be fast while the other is slow or even still. One of you might be on the floor while the other is standing. Play with all the different ways that the two of you can move very close, without touching.

Give them a little time to play with this.

Now, let that transition to touching lightly. Just barely feel your fingertips connect. Your touch is so light that it is like butterfly wings brushing against your partner's skin. Keep moving and play with all the different ways you can connect when you touch very, very lightly. You may have to slow down or you might not.

Give them some time to play with this, and experience how this light touch begins to change their understanding of their partner. If the music is beautiful they can do this for a long time.

Now slowly transition your light touching into pressing. Pressing as giving, not pushing. Give a little weight to your partner and receive a little weight from your partner, meeting each other in the middle. Pressing and moving and shifting your weight. You might try pressing hand to hand, back to back, or shoulder to shoulder, or shoulder to back.

Now press a little harder and a little deeper. See how far you and your partner want to take it, pressing as giving and meeting.

Give them a few moments to play with this.

Beautiful! Now, drop right back into touching lightly releasing all of the effort into an easy gentle connection with your partner. Butterfly wing touch. Breathe, and relax your jaw. Move together as if you were one organism, just breathing and moving and connecting lightly.

Give them a few moments.

And now back to moving as close as you can without touching at all. Feel the connection energetically between the two of you.

Give them a few moments.

Begin to slowly move away from your partner getting farther and farther away from each other, while still staying connected. Try to stay totally connected to your partner as you move across the room and get as far apart as you can.

Keep eye contact, feel the sense of your fingers touching. What do you have to do to keep connected when you are far away from each other? Dance as though there is nobody else in the room, just the two of you. When you are as far apart as you can get, find the end of your dance and come to stillness.

End by having them take a minute to share with each other. They will be happy to reunite.

Now, rejoin your partner and take a few minutes to share what happened for you in this exercise.

Facilitation Suggestions

In exercises that involve touch, it is always good to remind people to touch each other appropriately. Don't be afraid to address this subject. People will feel safer the minute you talk about it and talking about it usually prevents anything inappropriate from happening.

If you are worried about your group and touch, start by doing a little "touch and go" with your group. We have participants simply start moving thorough the room and as they are passing by each other gently and appropriately reach out and touch each other, and then the next person and the next, weaving some gentle connections in the group.

It is a fun and safe way to get present in the room, and to get warmed up for this more intimate exercise. You can also get a sense of your group and then you can establish norms for the group if they are needed.

At the end of the exercise, you can let the partners dance back to each other and finish when they reconnect. It is a different feeling than ending across the room, and sometimes you will feel like the group really needs to end connected.

Acknowledgement
We have used different versions of this exercise with hundreds of people since I first learned it from Nancy Spanier over twenty years ago.

Morning Practices

Finding a "Body Now" morning practice that fits for you, one where you tune in consciously every day to loving yourself is another direct path to wholeness and joy. I find I use different ones on different days, but still have my favorites, like "Never Ending Gratitude." These practices can be used any time of the day to return to your body and to return to love. Try them out and see which ones resonate for you.

Follow the general directions given or use the scripts, in italics, to guide a group through this exercise.

Never Ending Gratitude

Everything that you are aware of around you and inside you and in your spiritual and energetic field is a miracle in your life and is available for gratitude. This exercise, which is my personal favorite, is so much fun. Inspired by Ester and Jerry Hicks, it is guaranteed to make you smile. You can do it anywhere, any time. It lifts your spirits if they are down and reinforces your positive feelings in a heartbeat. I do this every morning as I drive down the mountain from my house into town, or as I take my morning shower, or as I make my morning tea. (Eight appreciations before breakfast!) It is so fun to keep coming up with new ways to be grateful.

Directions

Begin speaking—stream of consciousness—about all the things you are grateful for in your life, all the ways you appreciate yourself, all the ways you appreciate nature, the clothes you are wearing, your children and grandchildren, your friends, your brain, your body, your health, your organs, your heart, the house you live in, your neighbors, the post office, the grocery store, the road you are driving on, the car you are driving, the bus you are taking, whatever you think of. Keep going until you are tired, run out of things to say for the moment, or arrive at your destination.

Rocking In the Arms of Love

This is a great exercise to do while you are still lying in bed for a few moments before you begin your day, or just before you fall asleep at night. It is an important piece of the puzzle as we commit to the practice of loving ourselves.

If we had been raised believing that we were always being held and nurtured in the arms of the Great Mother or unconditionally loved by the Great Spirit, we would probably carry this feeling unconsciously with us all the time.

Directions
Lie down on your back and place your arms on your chest crossing over each other. Just lay them gently there and begin by feeling their presence. Focus on your hands and just let them send you loving energy—right down into your heart space.

As you begin to feel that energy radiating into your body, let yourself be aware of something that you know is beautiful about you, something that is deeply good about your essence. Just let a thought float up into your consciousness, and be there with that energy.

Take a breath and feel the Great Spirit holding you in her arms and rocking you back and forth, maybe you even hear her singing a soft chant to you. You might even sing or sound out loud to yourself. Your body loves the sound of your own voice.

As you are being rocked let your awareness float to all the ways you have loved and served in this life already, ways you have given to others from your own strengths and gifts. Notice all the little ways you show up in your life for others and see possibilities for them, and the ways you love those around you and the earth, the animals, the waters, the trees, the sky, the stars…

Now let your awareness float to all the ways you have received and accepted love in your life, all the ways you have let others into your heart. Notice the love that is there for you in your life right now and let it flow gently into your cells and move through your whole body, infusing your essence through your fluids.

Come back now to feeling the strong arms that are cradling you and rocking you and let yourself rest into that rocking, just letting go and resting deeply into the safety of those arms.

As you bring your awareness back into the room, move your body gently and slowly, rocking yourself up to sitting, and just notice how your body feels. Take your time. As you are ready, begin to see others in the room and connect a little with your eyes or your energy, just noticing how that is for you.

As the music begins to play, let your body move however it wants to move to the sacred music Jesse is playing. You might move a little or a lot, stay slow or maybe begin to move a little faster. Maybe you will play with someone else if you are in a group, or maybe just stay on your own. Take your time a to find your way back in to the room in your own way.

Inspired by the late Angeles Arrien.

A Sweet Little Dance of Joy

This is the simplest and quickest way I know to move into well-being and joy to start the day or anytime you need to refocus into the positive. Just tell your brain to do this and it will!

Directions

Pretend you are four or five years old and bounce around the room smiling and laughing and twirling and jumping around, doing a little dance of joy. Play with your own inner child or play with others if you are not alone. You can put some fun and joyful music on to get you going if you wish.

Body Sensations

This is the beginning of awakening to our bodies. It is also a great way to start the day. And it is a great place to return to if you are feeling disconnected or confused. Sensation pathways are a very reliable way to get back into your body, and you can easily coach yourself.

Directions

Scan your body for a place that feels good, focus on that place, give it attention, let it move, and see if it has any sound to express. Find another place that feels good. Let the two of them dance together and expand together.

Let the good feelings expand and grow as you keep seeking sensations that feel good and keep bringing them into your dance. Have fun just inviting your moving, happy, essence stream to move through you and around the room.

Notice how the positive energy spreads and grows as you keep giving attention to what feels good.

Turn Towards Your Heart

Every day in my early morning meditation, I check in to see if my heart is open, giving love to all, and to see if I need to let it flow to me, and to those around me more fully. If I find a place that is a little contracted, I release that stillness to flow again and feel immediately energized.

Tuning Your Heart

This is probably one of the quickest ways I have learned to come back into my body and get present with myself. You can do the first step of this without anyone around you knowing what you are doing, which can be helpful sometimes when I need to just quietly find me.

Begin by just placing your hand on your heart and letting your breath drop down into your heart so you are breathing in and out of your heart, just sensing the breath coming in through your heart and out through your heart. When you place your hand on your heart, oxytocin automatically begins to flow into your body, creating a sensation of feeling good.

Allow yourself to drop a little more into the breath just under your hand as you breathe in and out of your heart. You may want to cross your other hand over your heart as well to support the hand on your heart, or let your hand drop to your side if it is tired and just imagine it is still touching your heart.

Now let the people and animals and places on the earth that you love float up into your awareness, feeling your heart fill up with them, letting that energy ride into your awareness on your breath, which is gently going in and out of your heart.

Let yourself begin to hum to your heart, letting a soft ancient sound come through your body, humming a little sweet sound to your heart. Your heart loves the sound of your voice.

Just gently begin to hum and let your body tell you what to do next. Your body will take over and keep that connection to your open loving heart going, as you stay focused on the breath coming in and out and your sweet hum.

You may hum softly or loudly or on different tones or the same tone. Just let it unfold from your body, letting you body lead.

Slowly let the sound die away and come back to your breath and let your hand fall gently to your side, resting into the experience you just had for a few moments.

When you are ready you can blink your eyes open and see the room you are in and see your feet on the ground.

If you are doing this on your own, take a minute to check in with yourself and get fully present in the moment before heading into your day.

If you are in a group, this is a lovely thing to share about with a partner, enhancing each other's experience by revealing our own.

Inspired by a combination of HeartMath, Jean Houston, and Vickie Dodd.

Songs of Praise

The more we use all of our different modes of expression, like moving, writing, painting, drawing, dancing, singing, listening, smelling, and even just opening our eyes to new dimensions, the more engaged and excited our brain gets.

The writing exercise described below is another way to express praise that you can do every morning in your journal if you wish. A series of "sentence stem" prompts offers starting points for writing your own "Song of Praise." I have written at least 200 different praise songs over the last 12 years and still find them very satisfying and helpful when I want to tune into loving myself or need to reset my heart and soul. I have included a sample of one I wrote with the prompts highlighted in case it is helpful, but there is no right or wrong way to do this.

There are versions of the "sentence stem" prompts below for male writers and for female writers as well as one that is gender neutral. You can make copies of the one you want to use and copy some of the others if you are working with a group so they can choose which one they want to use.

When you are ready, find a quiet place to begin writing. As you are writing, keep changing your position as described below. If you want to stop at a certain time, be sure to set a timer so you can really drop all the way into the exercise and not worry about watching the time.

We will write for 20 minutes. If you are doing this exercise on your own, set a gentle sounding timer so you will know when to stop. Just fill in the sentence stems with your own answers. You could spend your whole time writing any one of these sentence stems or answer them all with only a few words or skip any that do not e resonate for you. This is your "Song of Praise," and you are in charge of how you want to manifest it.

Begin writing when you are ready, and as you are writing, keep changing your position a little or a lot. You could write lying on your back or belly or walking around the room or with your paper up on the wall. Or you could just uncross your legs or change the direction you are facing. I will remind you to change your body position a couple of times in the next 20 minutes.

Let's begin together. Close you eyes for a moment and notice any places in your body that need to release or relax a little, and send those places some warm, loving energy and support.

Now move around a little and take a deep breath and wiggle a little until you feel present. Begin writing as you are ready.

Facilitation Suggestions

If you wish to guide a group through this exercise, you may want to add an opportunity for sharing at the end of the script above. When we take the connections that we have made to ourselves and share them with others, we embrace our insights more fully. This process of revealing ourselves is the ground for all real connection with others, connection that opens our hearts, deepens our knowing, and enriches our lives.

A Song of Praise
For this Morning

My name is _____.

I am the daughter of _____ and

the granddaughter of _____and

the great-granddaughter of _____.

I sing my love and gratitude to the earth: to the waters, to the . . . .

I sound my deep spirit story and send blessings to . . . .

I thank my body for giving me . . . .

I praise my essence, (describe here) . . . .

I praise my unique contribution, (describe here) . . . .

I praise my beating heart and send love to . . . .

I call in my Grandparents, Ancestors, Teachers, Spirit Guides or . . . . today, and ask, with gratitude, for guidance around . . . .

A Song of Praise
For this Morning

My name is _____.

I am the son of _____ and

the grandson of _____and

the great-grandson of _____.

I sing my love and gratitude to the earth: to the waters, to the . . . .

I sound my deep spirit story and send blessings to . . . .

I thank my body for giving me . . . .

I praise my essence, (describe here) . . . .

I praise my unique contribution, (describe here) . . . .

I praise my beating heart and send love to . . . .

I call in my Grandparents, Ancestors, Teachers, Spirit Guides or . . . . today, and ask, with gratitude, for guidance around . . . .

A Song of Praise
For this Morning

My name is _____.

_____

_____

_____

I sing my love and gratitude to the earth: to the waters, to
the . . . .

I sound my deep spirit story and send blessings to . . . .

I thank my body for giving me . . . .

I praise my essence, (describe here) . . . .

I praise my unique contribution, (describe here) . . . .

I praise my beating heart and send love to . . . .

I call in my Grandparents, Ancestors, Teachers, Spirit
Guides or . . . . today, and ask, with gratitude, for guidance
around . . . .

A Sample Song of Praise

My name is Alana. I am the daughter of Helen Leora, the granddaughter of Ruby Kincaid, and the great-grand daughter of Lena Browning. I am the Mother of Matthew, Andrea, Cassandra, Norah, Lucas, Aaron, and Morgan. I am the grandmother of Tobias, Jayda, Lila, Elias, Benjamin, Margaret, Caitlin, and Sage.

I sing my love and gratitude to the earth: to the waters, to the trees, to the birds and the winds, to the warmth of the sun and the wisdom of the moon.

I sound my deep spirit story and send blessings to my children and their children as they stand in their truth and reach for new ways to live and love together.

I thank my body for giving me health and serving me in my work, bringing me lots of good energy, and strength.

I praise my essence, which guides me in tenderness to manifest my authentic self and live my own soul's journey.

I praise my beating heart and send love to all the children of the earth.

I praise my unique contribution, which I will happily bring to everyone who wants to dance and laugh and play and live in joy with me.

I call in my Spirit Guides today, and ask, with gratitude, for guidance in stepping more fully and courageously into my self, and showing up 100% in every moment.

Out Loud Praise for the Earth and for Yourself

This is a very old and basic shamanistic practice that is common in slightly different variations in many different cultures and tribal groups. The shaman or spiritual guide of the tribe begins the day with a song of praise for the ancestors, the earth, and all the spirit beings that guide life. In some groups the whole community does this together in a ritual form they all are familiar with.

Either way, it is a powerful way to ground yourself in gratitude as you begin your day, remembering all that is there to hold you and support you. I like to take it one more step and think of myself as a member of a tribe and praise myself for what I will bring to my tribe, as the day unfolds.

Directions
Go out on your deck or in your front yard or stand where you can look out the window, or imagine a window for yourself looking at whatever pleases you and, speaking out loud, begin to praise the earth in every way you can think of, from the flowers that you see in your garden to the piles of snow in your driveway, to the trees in the park nearby.

Praise what you can't see in the moment also, like the high mountains or the rhythms of the ocean waves, or wild meadows filled with fragrant yellow flowers.

Praise your ancestors and thank them for your life here on the beautiful earth.

Finally, praise yourself for the love and service you will bring to the earth this day.

When you feel complete, you can continue on with "Never Ending Gratitude" or write a "Song of Praise" if you have a little more time.

Meditation—Any and All Forms

Meditation takes us to a place of loving kindness towards ourselves. We drop into a place of touching our essence energy, our life force, and we rest our minds into allowing the moment to be just as it is.

Some people meditate in formal postures and with specific chants that they have learned from teachers, which is great. As the practice of quieting the mind has evolved, many other ways to meditate have shown up, and this, like everything else, is very personal.

We know that everyone can access a state of quiet peacefulness, which is both calm and joyful. You just need to find a regular time to tune into this quiet each day and stick with it for two weeks. Once you experience the enormous benefits from this kind of space in your life you will happily find the time each day. Below are some possible choices to experiment with and combine as you wish.

Improvised Meditation

I am sure it is not surprising to you that this is my favorite form of meditation, both for me and for you, and this is why. Research has established that lively, spontaneous activity is the most important key to a healthy brain. And since everything we do depends on a healthy brain, it just seems like a good idea to keep making space for our improvised spontaneous selves to show up.

What I mean by an improvised meditation is that I respond in the moment to what my body and soul most need, and as that changes I follow my body's lead.

For example, I might start my evening meditation lighting candles and incense at my altar, and then sitting quietly and tuning into my breath. Then I stay open to what my body sensations are telling me and see what wants to happen next.

Maybe I will want to sing or chant or sound as I sit, or let movement follow my breath and my sound. Maybe I will want to lie down or walk. From that state of quieted mind where I began, my body will lead me if I am listening.

Another time, I might start my meditation painting from a sort of stream of consciousness place, letting the flow of the paint and the water and color take me deep into a dream state. I might draw a tarot card to start and let that message start my meditation. I might begin with a stream of "Never Ending Gratitude" or begin by dancing and singing.

I might take myself into a meadow in my mind or to the top of a mountain and rest into that environment as I breathe and move or just as I sit at my altar. There are as many variations as there are bodies. Have fun experimenting with all different ways to come to a quiet, embodied place and to see what wants to happen from one moment to the next moment.

Walking Meditation

I learned a specific set of visualizations for this, but again I want to emphasize that you can do this your own way, including just walking anywhere while focusing your consciousness on each step you take. Below is the adaptation I use sometimes for my practice. I walk in a clockwise circle around my room, as that is the way I can keep a continuous, smooth path going.

Begin by dropping your energy down through your feet all the way into the center of the earth. Feel how the earth comes up to meet your feet, supporting you and receiving your consciousness. Now let the top of your head open to the energy from the heavens and feel the line running down through the center of your body, like a plumb line, from the heavens to the earth and back up again.

Slowly begin walking, taking small steps and breathe in on your first step and out on your second, continuing this pattern for the duration of your walk. If it is comfortable for you, breathe in and out through your nose.

Just keep moving gently, relaxing into the rhythm of your walking and breathing: breathing in and stepping and breathing out and stepping.

Continue your walk, and now imagine that each time you step down, you are kissing the ground with love with your foot. And imagine that each time you lift your foot off the ground, a white lotus flower of peace blooms where you just stepped. Just keep walking and breathing feeling your kiss on the ground and seeing the flowers blooming in your path.

Come back to your easy breath and the rhythm of your walking right now, letting go of any set patterns, and relax even more into the kissing and the blooming. In this moment, all is well.

Inspired by a method taught by Thich Nhat Hanh.

Standing Meditation
I learned this from a wonderful dance teacher at the Colorado Dance Festival in the nineties. It is a simple and powerful way to get reconnected to your body and your breath. I often do this just as I step out of my bed in the morning, giving myself a quiet moment to find my center.

It is also a great way to gather yourself up after the end of a long day and to get centered before going to sleep. I have even done a modified version of this while standing in a long line to make good use of the time and avoid wasting my energy with impatience.

Before beginning set a timer for 10 minutes, making sure the sound of the timer is gentle and not too loud.

Stand with your feet comfortably apart with your knees slightly softened and your weight dropped into your feet. Relax your jaw and your belly, and gently allow space to open up in your body. Just let your hands hang gently by your sides with your fingers relaxed and let your breath be natural.

Come to stillness, maybe feeling yourself as a rock on the earth, and just be there. The timer signals your ten minutes is up. Slowly begin to move in any way your body guides you. You can make sound with your movement if you wish, as you slowly come back into the room.

Lying Down

This is a great way to begin your morning before you even get out of bed. Taking 15 minutes to relax into yourself before entering your day of interactions is an invaluable gift you can give yourself. This is also a great way to restore your energy in the afternoon or after a particularly stressful interaction. Fifteen minutes of this kind of deep rest is plenty to get you back on track.

Sometimes I like to put on some kind of meditative music for this and focus on the sounds of the music and how they vibrate through my body, which is just enough outside sound to keep me from slipping into sleep.

Lay on your back with you knees bent and slightly apart, your hands resting on your stomach or down along your sides. Let your knees rest inward toward each other until they touch if this is more comfortable for you. Let's begin with some deep breaths. Just relax into your body and tune into your breath, breathing in and out your nose, maybe even counting six counts in and six counts out for each breath to help you transition out of your day's activities.

Now just let your breath return to normal, and drop your consciousness inside your body, noticing your heartbeat, sensing all your organs piled up there together and let yourself rest into a state of gratitude for the miracle of those organs and your body and they way it all works together. Just breathe easily and keep listening to your body and the little sounds it makes, the rhythms or your breath and heartbeat, and relax into the mystery of it all.

Word Games

For some participants, working with words is a great break from all the moving and breathing. We have gathered a huge collection of positive, evolving words from magazines and lists we make for our groups to use to create spontaneous poetry, make hourly nametags, add to art projects, write appreciations for each other, land promises, and use as inspiration and reminders.

Making the Word Pool

Start by cutting single manifestation words out of all kinds of magazines—being sure they are all positive and supportive in their direction. You want just one word in each cutting, since the exercises we play with the words work better if you have single words and not phrases. You want to collect words that stand alone and evoke an image or a feeling, not the little connectors (like *it* or *the*) or pronouns. Yoga and dance magazines are good sources for positive manifestation words, and you will find them everywhere once you start looking. You can also make your own lists of words to add in to the pot, maybe varying the typefaces and type colors.

In order to have a collection that you can use again, you can glue these beautiful words, which are all different sizes and colors, onto a piece of white paper and photocopy them. Then make several copies of each sheet that you and your group have created so you have plenty to cut out for the games. If you keep a master copy you can add more sheets to your collection as time goes on.

Now you take your sheets you have copied and cut out the words you have copied so you have piles and piles of individual words to play some of the games listed below or make up your own.

Word Poems

Materials
Words

These are the "Word Pool" words you have cut out as described above.

Pretty Paper

This is for the background. It can be solid colored cardstock, 8 1/2 x 11, or fancier paper if you wish. Single sheets of all different kinds of paper and scrapbooking tablets are available at JoAnn's and Michael's.

Glue Sticks

Feathers

We sometimes provide feathers of all different colors to add a little whimsy to this project. They glue on easily with the glue sticks.

Directions

This is a great exercise for a change of pace and some rest from physical moving. It also lets your group fall back into using words, which can be very comforting.

Begin by placing all the words out on the floor face down. Then each person draws five words from the pot without looking at what they are drawing. We have so many words now we can't put them all face down so we just ask people to draw without looking. Sometimes I have the group draw ten words, as they seem to need more words. Another variation is to let them draw some words not looking and then go back and choose some consciously.

Then invite your group to arrange those words into a little poem, trying some different arrangements. When they are ready, they can glue them down however they want on their paper (and add some feathers or other decorations if they wish).

We often use this game when we are seeking an answer from the universe, or from our higher selves, like a waking dream experience. Or we use it as a part of another exploration we are engaged in, like asking what the ancestors have to say, or asking for guidance in the next step on our "Walking the Path Forward" journey, or asking what needs more love in ourselves in our "Walking the Path of Self Love" exercise.

Be sure to share all the poems at the end—walk around looking at them and appreciating them. They are always remarkable little pieces of magic. I usually have people find a partner when they are finished and share one-on-one while they are waiting for everybody to complete their poems.

Acknowledgement
I first learned to use words in this way from Nancy Spanier, who had an incredible collection of words that she had made. She used them as inspiration for making movement sequences, or as text that could be spoken into dance sequences.

Collage Poetry

Materials
Magazines
For cutting out pictures, words, and phrases.
Pretty Paper
This is for the background. It can be solid colored cardstock, 8 1/2 x 11, or fancier paper if you wish. Single sheets of all different kinds of paper and scrapbooking tablets are available at JoAnn's and Michael's.
Glue Sticks

Directions
These collages combine words and images to create poetry. Participants begin by cutting words and phrases and pictures (if they wish) that they are particularly drawn to out of magazines. They choose as many images and words or phases as they want and then arranged them into a poem. They may also add in little words that they write themselves. After they glue the words and images all down onto beautiful paper, and they share their collage poem with the group or with a partner. You will be amazed at the beauty and depth of these poems.

Acknowledgement
Our wonderful creative facilitator, Dodi, created this idea in her collage poetry classes at our summer workshop.

Personal Nametags for the Moment

Materials
Words

Theses are the words you have cut out as described above.
Pretty Paper

This is for the background. It can be solid colored cardstock, 8 1/2 x 11, or fancier paper if you wish. Single sheets of all different kinds of paper and scrapbooking tablets are available at JoAnn's and Michael's.
Glue Sticks

Directions
We often start our workshops using the word pool words to make nametags. It is a magical way to encourage your group to practice tuning in to how they are feeling in the moment and to share those feelings. So instead of putting your actual name on the nametag, you put the word or words that describe who you are right now. This is a great way to encourage a culture of revealing and sharing right from the start—and it's fun.

Choosing positive words to describe yourself feels good. Then you get to glue those words on a background and pin them on and walk around being seen! And the bonus is that you are directing people to what you would like them to see in you right now.

We encourage the participants to change their nametags as the day goes on—maybe during a break or during lunch, playing again with the idea of what is happening in this moment inside themselves.

You need to have plenty of glue sticks and safety pins on the table and pre-cut rectangles (or other shapes) of paper for the participants to glue their words on. It is fun to use papers that are patterned and pretty for these background squares so making a nametag is a pleasing visual experience as well.

For some reason—maybe childhood memories—gluing is something most everybody likes to do. And our participants pin these on their clothing in all different places – sometimes related to their words and sometimes just for fun.

Appreciation Nametags Variation

Another way we use these words in our workshops is to have people make nametags for somebody else in the room using words that indicate things they appreciate about that person. We put all the names of our participants each day in a basket and everybody draws one person to do an appreciation nametag for. This way nobody gets left out and we all get to see and know new people we might not have connected to.

Inspired by Susan Goldsmith Wooldridge, "Poemcrazy."

Music Resources

Follow the links below to find available recordings by some of the extraordinary musicians who have worked with us at Turning the Wheel.

Jesse Manno

spot.colorado.edu/~manno/contact.html

Recommended Recordings

Sea Spirits

Lazer Vaudeville

Rainforest

Vickie Dodd

www.sacredsoundschool.com

Recommended Recording

Rest Assured(with James Hoskins on cello)

Resonance Meditations

David Willey

http://www.generalrubric.com/hamster/main.html

Recommended Recordings

Songs from the Hamster Theatre

Carnival Detournement

Find Collection of Songs for Community
Singing at www.turningthewheel.org/songs

About the Author

Alana Shaw, founder and executive director of Turning the Wheel, is an inspiring and empowering speaker, teacher, and guide. Alana has facilitated joyful and healing movement events in cities in the US and Canada for over 30 years. Her dynamic and energetic presentation style is both humorous and transforming, and consistently positive and uplifting for her audiences.

In addition to building community and nurturing leadership and self expression in children of all ages and abilities in the schools, Alana has also trained hundreds of teachers and students in her "Body Now" model for creating sustainable change in their lives and their careers.

She holds an MFA is Dance from the University of Colorado with a thesis on healing and reintegration through creative expression, and is the author of "Dancing Our Way Home," a 406¬ page book of exercises, stories and wisdom. (Available on Amazon)

When she is not traveling and working with youth and educators around the country, Alana lives in the mountains above Boulder, CO. Her greatest joy and wisest teachers are her seven children and eight grandchildren.

> "Everything we do in Turning the Wheel is an attempt to come back into relationship with our interdependence as human beings, and with the need for love, not power, to form the basis for how we live on the earth. We are passionately committed to building and sustaining transformative communities that are inclusive of all people, and that reach for and model unconditional love and acceptance as the norm."

> —Alana Shaw

Printed in the United States
By Bookmasters